"One of the most encouraging signs of renewed vigor in the church today is the return to the biblical story as the framework of our theology. To my knowledge, *Chaos and Grace* is the first story-framed study of the wonderful themes of the liberating presence of God's Spirit—from Genesis to Revelation we get Spirit, Spirit, Spirit, and where the Spirit is, there is freedom. Be careful. When the Spirit comes we encounter a liberating chaos."

—**Scot McKnight**, Karl A. Olsson Professor in Religious Studies, North Park University; author of *One.Life: Jesus Calls, We Follow*

"Mark Galli calls the church to awake to the Spirit of God—the Spirit who cannot be programmed, coerced, or manipulated. The Spirit who liberates us from such activities and invites us to deeper, more unexpected relationship with God. This book will challenge the way you think about the church in America."

—**Margaret Feinberg**, www.margaretfeinberg.com; author of *Scouting the Divine* and *The Organic God*

"When he writes or speaks, Mark always makes me think and wrestle with issues—generally mine! This book wasn't written for a fast, casual read. You will have to slow down and reflect. Some chapters you will need to go back and reread more than once. Biblical, solid, and honest—it will force you not just to think but to examine yourself."

—**Bob Roberts Jr.**, senior pastor, NorthWood Church; author of *Transformation* and *Glocalization*

"Mark Galli's *Chaos and Grace* reflects his mature views after many years of editing *Christianity Today*. Using biblical references applied to the present church scene, he shows the crucial value of the Holy Spirit's 'power of disorder' as contrasted to the comfortable and easy life of many modern churches. This is a most valuable resource for pastors of all types of churches, from small congregations to megachurches. I highly recommend it."

—**Vinson Synan,** dean emeritus,
Regent University School of Divinity

"Mark Galli has had it with the idea that life can be controlled or in any way managed. He's yearning for Jesus to really *mean* freedom. Galli observes the entry of the Holy Spirit into biblical history as a chaos-creating dismantling of useless supports. He counsels giving up rather than trying harder, an end to projects of transformation in favor of grace and mercy toward what is. We all want liberation from personal repetitions and bad habits. Mark Galli pinpoints this liberation in our shattering moments of giving in to God's upsetting intrusions. Call this a 'theology of liberation' for evangelicals!"

—**Paul F. M. Zahl,** former dean and president,
Trinity School for Ministry; author of
Grace in Practice: A Theology of Everyday Life

"As a human suffering from the control addiction that Mark Galli so saliently describes, I found *Chaos and Grace* disturbing, upsetting, and disrupting. With unrelenting clarity, Galli points to dozens of biblical and contemporary examples of a liberating God using chaos and disorder to break our bonds of self-direction and plunge us into the disorienting freedom of grace. I finished this book shaken; the more I ponder what I've read, the more I suspect that the things it left rattled are my chains."

—**Carolyn Arends,** recording artist and author

CHAOS
and *Grace*

DISCOVERING THE LIBERATING

WORK OF THE HOLY SPIRIT

MARK GALLI

BakerBooks

a division of Baker Publishing Group
Grand Rapids, Michigan

© 2011 by Mark Galli

Published by Baker Books
a division of Baker Publishing Group
P.O. Box 6287, Grand Rapids, MI 49516-6287
www.bakerbooks.com

Printed in the United States of America

Library of Congress Cataloging-in-Publication Data
Galli, Mark.
    Chaos and grace : discovering the liberating work of the Holy Spirit / Mark Galli.
        p.   cm.
    Includes bibliographical references (p.   ).
    ISBN 978-0-8010-1350-8 (cloth)
    1. Church renewal. 2. Liberty—Religious aspects—Christianity. 3. Grace (Theology) 4. God (Christianity) 5. Holy Spirit. I. Title.
    BV600.G35 2011
    262.0017—dc22   2011014733

11   12   13   14   15   16   17   7   6   5   4   3   2   1

In keeping with biblical principles of creation stewardship, Baker Publishing Group advocates the responsible use of our natural resources. As a member of the Green Press Initiative, our company uses recycled paper when possible. The text paper of this book is composed in part of post-consumer waste.

To David and Ted, colleagues and friends.

CONTENTS

Contents

William H. Willimon

I recently participated in a congregational self-study of a church that's in trouble. Once a vital church in the heart of a thriving city, the congregation is now a small group of people fighting for its institutional life amid urban decay and decline, a little island of neo-Gothic sacredness surrounded by the city's chaos.

One of the exercises we engaged in was a "SWOT analysis," whereby we were asked to identify congregational strengths, weaknesses, opportunities, and threats. We sailed through the first three items; this congregation, for all of its difficulties, is blessed with many gifts for ministry. When we got to the last item on the list—threats—one could feel the tension rising in the room. Hesitantly, somberly, we began to list the threats, fearsome dangers that nobody really wanted to talk about: a neighborhood with declining population, shrinking financial resources, an aging building, security concerns. The spiritual energy seeped out of the room; the fear was palpable.

And then someone said, "God. Be sure to put God on the list."

What? God? A threat?

She explained, "As the church, let's remember that the biggest threat to our stability, our comfort, and our self-confidence is God. We serve a living God who just won't leave us alone, who keeps giving us impossible assignments, and who refuses to let us die a quiet, peaceful death."

Wow. She either had been drinking some theologically laced Kool-Aid or had been reading an advance copy of Mark Galli's *Chaos and Grace*. Mark knows that of all the challenges faced by Christians today, the greatest challenge is our oldest: to keep up with the wild machinations and ridiculous demands of a true and living God who refuses to leave us alone.

God knows we try. We've got our self-help pop psychologies, our religious rites and latest denominational programs, our successful megachurches and their good-looking preachers, our insatiable lust for pain-free, boringly bourgeois lives—all as our attempts to ward off God's disruptive determination to save us from ourselves. The good news is that the Holy Spirit is relentless. There is hope for us yet.

With great winsomeness and wit, Mark gives us a fast-paced, hard-hitting narrative that manages to tag most of our Christian sins while reminding us of the core testimonial of our faith. We are saved by grace, not by our righteousness, in order that we might, through grace, be truly righteous. As editor of the prestigious *Christianity Today*, Mark has a unique vantage point from which to observe our sinful corporate and personal shenanigans. With great grace, he nails us. Then Mark reminds us of the imperishable witness with which we have been entrusted. This makes *Chaos and Grace* something rare and wonderful—a book that manages not only to tell hard Christian truth but also to stir up real Christian hope.

For contemporary Christians, Mark's book will be a both truthful and hopeful gift. The gospel is indeed strong enough to deal with the assorted chaos in which we live, and the Trinity loves us graciously enough to engender that graceful chaos that pushes us closer to God. I've read few expositions of the faith that manage to embody in so warm and accessible a way theologian Karl Barth's assertion that the grace of God is always experienced by us entrenched sinners as disruption and dislocation. *Chaos and Grace* is a grand invitation to experience again, as if for the first time, the adventure of life lived in the light of a God who, in Christ Jesus, manages to be not only demanding but also gracious, graciously giving us all we need to be faithful in chaotic times.

Eberhard Busch reports that back in the sixties there was a brilliant lecture in Tübingen, Germany, by Joseph Ratzinger (later a cardinal, now the pope) in which Ratzinger extolled the grand and glorious virtues of his one, true, holy Catholic Church. At the end of the lecture Karl Barth asked "humbly" how Ratzinger could be sure that his "magnificent church," for all its grand rites and good works, was "not a clever escape from the Holy Spirit." Barth's question caused Ratzinger to fumble and set off some chaotic rumblings throughout the audience.

I wish old Barth was still around. I think he would have liked Mark's book.

William H. Willimon
Bishop, the United Methodist Church,
North Alabama Conference

ACKNOWLEDGMENTS

As I suggest in the introduction, it is now impossible for me to recognize who has been most instrumental in the making of this book. Where did I get the idea that chaos could be a source of grace? That freedom is core to the life of faith? That the Holy Spirit is one who prods and unsettles as much as consoles and comforts? Which of the ideas in this book offer something new, and which are mere retelling of old truths? In much of this, I have little idea. I have walked the earth too many years, met too many people, read too many books to know where many of my ideas come from and, most importantly, who to thank. Just when I imagine I've come up with a fresh idea, I run across an underlined passage in a book years I read years earlier that says the same thing, or a friend reminds me of a conversation in which we debated the idea long ago!

Yet a few things are concrete and clear. The Church of the Resurrection in Glen Ellyn has deepened my understanding and experience of the Holy Spirit in extraordinary ways.

Bob Hosack and Wendy Wetzel, my editors, have been patient and helpful, as usual, as I've missed deadlines and struggled to give shape to this book.

A number of people read a final draft and gave me wise feedback, in particular Leslie Leyland Fields, Scot McKnight, Kirsten Guidero, David Neff, and Ted Olsen. The latter two gentlemen are extraordinarily gifted journalists and thinkers with whom I have the privilege of working daily, and their shaping of my thought over the years has been incalculable.

The readers of my Soulwork columns, especially those who have taken the trouble to comment or email me, have helped sharpen the column—some of which has found its way here—and thus this book.

I'm also grateful to members of the Randy Smith Sunday school class of Houston's St. Luke's Methodist Church, who listened as I presented an early version of these themes and were nonetheless gracious and encouraging!

Finally, my wife, Barbara, gave the manuscript a careful read and saved me from many a blunder and much reader confusion. As usual, her presence is felt in every page. I may not follow all her suggestions, but nothing I write is crafted without wrestling with her concerns. Over many happy years of marriage, she has been, in addition to her other wifely roles, a formidable intellectual sparring partner who has made me not just a better writer but a better person.

I used to play a game with friends in which we'd start by one of us shutting our eyes. Then the others would spin the person round and round. After we were sure he was good and dizzy, he'd open his eyes and attempt to walk a straight line to another friend some twenty feet away. But of course, this is impossible. Your equilibrium is destroyed, and while your mind tells you to step forward, your whole body leans sharply to one side. You look and feel like a drunk, because you simply cannot walk in a straight line. Everything is confused and chaotic. Soon you lose your balance and fall. All the while, you and your friends are laughing so hard no one can speak.

This is what holy chaos can be like: a life chaotic and confused. We feel like we're walking like a drunk. Sometimes we laugh to the point of tears; sometimes we cry to the point of despair. It's a life of freedom, but a sometimes frightening freedom. It's a life of joy, but not the happy-clappy kind. More of a confident sense of inner purpose amidst the confusion.

This is not what most people think of when they think of the Christian life. They often see activity and earnest intensity rather than a calming joy. More furrowed brows

15

than welcoming arms. More grumbling about what's wrong with the culture than entering with abandon into the world God created and loves. You know something is the matter when we Christians have to be lectured to be more joyful and welcoming.

As much as we yearn for freedom, freedom makes us nervous. We read the apostle Paul's magnificent announcement—"For freedom Christ has set us free" (Gal. 5:1)—and we smile. But we also shake our heads, having little idea what that really means. At face value, it sounds like a formula for moral anarchy. And we're pretty sure religion is not about that.

I think what Paul means is simple: God meets us daily with unbounded grace, and as a result, we have unimaginable opportunities to love and to serve a deeply troubled world. This is so counterintuitive, we refuse to believe it, and so we settle for mere religion—where things are a bit more predictable and under some measure of control. Religion seems a much more edifying experience than a relationship with the Holy Spirit.

In talking about religion, I don't mean the legalism of prim Puritans of the past or fundamentalists of the present. I'm talking about well-intentioned church leaders who regularly trade in trust in the Holy Spirit's leading for mere church growth principles. And sincere parachurch execs who prefer to manage by the minute rather than pray unceasingly. And earnest marketers anxious to control the brand of their church. And postmodern evangelists who assure us, sometimes dogmatically and judgmentally, that modernism is both evil and dead. And compassionate political activists left and right who imply that we cannot justify our existence without joining their cause. And culture warriors who tell us to take up arms. And frustrated pastors who scold their congregations for lack of commitment. And bored parishioners who get their kicks by manipulating the church board to ensure that the nursery is painted yellow and not green.

I sometimes talk as if the problem is out there. But an honest look at our hearts says otherwise. When I've mentioned to friends that I was writing a book about how the Spirit wants to free us from addiction to religion, a number have told me to hurry up and write the book, for this is just the book they need. When we look within, we see the chasm between the dynamic life the New Testament pictures and the drudgery and smallness that seem to characterize our own. Worship and prayer have indeed become spiritual *disciplines*, more a matter of duty than delight. We manage our "profiles"—on Facebook and off—with great care to make sure others have a good impression of our spirituality, but the effort is wearing us down. We want to take up the cause of the poor and oppressed, but we are afraid of giving up our comforts. Most of us are tired of being merely "good Christians." We suspect there is more, but we're not quite sure how to take hold of it.

The tension is most taut when we are confronted with chaos and confusion. You cannot live and not confront such. But who among us hasn't figured out a variety of coping mechanisms to avoid the pain they cause?

The late Walter Martin was a Christian apologist who specialized in ministry to people involved in alternative religions—Mormons, Jehovah's Witnesses, and the like. He used to tell the story of a conversation he'd had with a woman who assured him she had found the secret to dealing effectively with Jehovah's Witnesses. Martin was gracious. He said he had been debating Jehovah's Witnesses for years and was always looking for ways to minister to them more effectively.

"Well," she said enthusiastically, "when I see them coming up my driveway, I shut the blinds and lock my door, and when they knock, I pretend I'm not home!"

When chaos comes knocking on our door, we use religion to shut out the intruder. Prayer becomes merely a means of comfort; worship, a spring of inspiration; and Bible reading, a source of encouragement. To be sure, if the Christian faith doesn't bring comfort, inspiration, and encouragement, we are just playing games. But Christ has come to offer us more than merely a religion of comfort and encouragement.

Instead, he's given us the Holy Spirit—the most unsettling gift imaginable, for this is the gift that brings both chaos and grace.

If the world has forgotten God, as Alexander Solzhenitsyn said, it's also true that Christians have as well. More to the point, we've forgotten the God of the Bible—the untamable, unruly, mysterious Spirit who regularly upsets our plans and, yes, sometimes creates havoc in our lives. We've become blind to this God, and when he works his chaos among us, we think it's either the devil or blind chance. No wonder we shut the curtains and pretend we're not home!

In preparing this book, I was fascinated as I read in Scripture how time and again God introduced chaos into the life of his people: the call of Abraham to leave the comforts of Ur; the call of Moses to abandon his bucolic life and become a political revolutionary; the challenge to Gideon to abandon the security of superior forces; the call of Israel to sojourn in the desert; the exile of God's people to a foreign land; the "mean and wild" ministry of Jesus; the strange event of Pentecost; the conversion of Saul—to name but a few chaotic moments in salvation history.

A closer look reveals not a capricious God, but one who uses chaos to liberate us from mere religion, from addiction to order and control, to something much more interesting.

What the alcoholic does with drink is what many Christians do with religion. Religion becomes a means of sometimes avoiding and sometimes trying to control chaos. But religion, like alcohol, often makes us numb. And sometimes it makes things worse. Naturally, this only prompts us to drink more of religion! The cycle continues in a downward spiral of chaos and confusion—until we accept that we really are out of control and that the only hope is to abandon control. That's when the life of freedom becomes a real possibility.

We normally think God is to be found in peace and order, and this is true. But I hope to show that he can also be found in disorder and confusion—and that often he is the instigator of the chaos.

~~~

After an opening chapter on a key challenge for the church today, I will use the first half of this book to sketch in narrative fashion the themes of chaos and liberation as they are found in the Bible. I admit that in some ways this is a quirky reading of Scripture, for other themes are arguably more important: covenant, grace, salvation, the people of God, and so forth. Then again, liberation is no small theme, and one I believe needs to be revisited in our time, though without all the Marxist baggage of what is called liberation theology.

These chapters are theological and narrative in nature. As Walter Brueggemann says of the opening chapters of Genesis, "Our exposition will insist that these texts be taken neither as history nor as myth. Rather, we insist that the text is a *proclamation* of God's decisive dealing with his creation."[1] My exposition is grounded, I trust, in forty years of Bible reading and reflects something of the biblical commentaries and monographs I've read over the years. The older I get, the more I realize that there is nothing I write that has not been said before. The problem is that I often have no idea any longer which book or speaker has influenced specific insights. But the reader can be assured that my seeming lack of giving credit is not a way of saying these are my own thoughts. They are decidedly not, but from whence many of them came remains a mystery to me.

I've also become increasingly convinced that the historical-critical method in which I've been schooled is not as fruitful as is a theological and especially a Christocentric reading of Scripture. So I don't spend a lot of time exegeting the text in a way that has now become more or less expected and traditional—with a discussion of sources, structure, word derivations, and the like. Unfortunately, many times the historical-critical method (with its various "rules" for "sound" interpretation), for all its benefits, is another way we try to control divine things and bring order to the Spirit's unruly freedom. (See Søren Kierkegaard's take on this in his delightful essay "Kill the Commentators."[2]) Narrative theology, on the other hand, cannot be so easily controlled.

Thus it is precisely the character of narrative theology that demands that it be used in this book. A carefully controlled, exegetical treatise would by its very nature contradict what I'm driving at. It would compel the reader by rules of interpretation and strict logic that he or she has to buy into the idea of freedom—as if that method could truly offer freedom.

Instead, I proceed more narratively—with all the ambiguity and confusion that this includes. Naturally, I am making an argument that I hope will convince and does not abuse or misuse the biblical witness. But I aim to convince not with detailed exegesis but by a kind of intuitive reasoning that in the end makes sense of the overall teaching of Scripture. One cannot be coerced intellectually into a life of freedom. It has to come as a gift of the Spirit, who persuades not just through the strictures of careful argument but also through the dynamics of narrative.

The second half of the book is my analysis of current church culture. The analysis is driven by my reading of the Acts of the Apostles—the biblical book where the Spirit invades the world with holy chaos and freedom. The examination is by no means thorough or systematic, though I have made use of the insights of a number of commentaries.[3] I've popped into the book of Acts at moments when the Spirit was doing things that seem most counterintuitive to our age. But I've tried to ensure that my reading of these moments accords with the flow and theme of the entire book.

20

This biblical analysis is informed by my observations as senior managing editor of *Christianity Today*. From this perch I see more than most what is going on in the contemporary church. To paraphrase theologian Karl Barth, this second part of the book is an attempt to think with the Bible in one hand and the magazine in the other. Anyone who knows my writing (a number of these chapters have been adapted from my online column, SoulWork) will see that I am in my own way trying to introduce a little holy chaos into the situation. Whether this is of the Spirit, the reader must judge.

In any case, I hope that this admittedly personal attempt to listen to the Spirit will, at least here and there, resonate with readers. I hope that they will find themselves startled into moments of confusion, and at other times glimpse the radical freedom the Spirit is creating in and for them. Maybe they'll know moments when they find themselves stretched out on the ground, overcome with dizziness and maybe even laughter. And when the laughter dies down, they'll pick themselves up and, rather than merely rejoin the religious life, give themselves to the world for whom Christ died.

Mark Galli

1

THE RELIGIOUS CAPTIVITY OF THE CHURCH

I begin with the philosophy of pornographer Larry Flynt, founder of *Hustler* magazine. Mr. Flynt is not known for his brilliance or wisdom, but as they say, even a broken clock is right twice a day. Regarding religion he said something prosaic but largely true: "Religion has caused more harm than any other idea since the beginning of time."[1] Since religion traffics in the deepest mysteries of metaphysics and morals, and since it is taught, learned, and practiced by sinful human beings—well, we shouldn't be surprised that the combination can be lethal sometimes.

In this book, I hope to show how the Christian faith is fundamentally different than religion—religion understood as our attempt to order and control our lives before God. But this is no screed against religion as such, for there are dimensions of religion—its rituals, moral codes, community structure, and so forth—that we cannot live without.

This salutary function of religion has been noted recently by various and sundry scholars, like Bruce Sheiman. After a recent spate of atheist-authored books decrying religion, he wrote the contrarian *An Atheist Defends Religion: Why Humanity Is Better Off with Religion than Without It*.[2] He argued that religion helps people live happier and healthier lives by giving them meaning and purpose; it benefits society enormously by establishing food closets and hospitals and rescue missions. As the subtitle says, all told, humanity is better off because of religion.

The social value of religion was again noted at a 2009 conference of journalists organized by the Pew Forum on Religion and Public Life. At that conference, Robert Putnam outlined the conclusions of a book he and coauthor David E. Campbell were working on called *American Grace: How Religion Divides and Unites Us*.[3] Putnam, the author of *Bowling Alone: The Collapse and Revival of American Community*, is a leading academic expert on American religious and civic life. And "Campbell is his rising heir," according to Michael Gerson, who summarized this conference in his column in the *Washington Post*.[4]

Contrary to assumptions of hard-core secularists, Putnam said that "Religious Americans are nicer, happier, and better citizens." They are more generous with their time and money, and they give not only to religious but also to secular causes. They tend to join more voluntary associations and attend more public meetings. All in all, religious Americans are three to four times more socially engaged than those who remain unaffiliated.

"Theology is not the predictor of civic behavior; being part of a community is," wrote Gerson as he summarized Putnam and Campbell's book. Christianity may not be the only socially useful religion, but it is clearly a very effective one, garnering adherents from 33 percent of the world. As a *religion*, Christianity is very much a human enterprise, and a successful one at that—even if the keys to its success can be understood in very human ways.

For example, the principles that have helped American evangelicals become a successful social institution are no mystical secret, available only to the initiated. Church administrators look to business gurus to discover how to manage large organizations like megachurches. Small group leaders ponder social psychology to discover principles that will help groups become more intimate. Christian educators utilize the latest pedagogies to inform their teaching. Worship leaders employ large group dynamics to determine how to use music and prayer to move people into a worshipful mood and send them forth uplifted. Pastors study rhetoric to make their sermons pop. Look at any successful, growing church, and you'll find it uses principles common to any well-managed group or organization.

Such wisdom is the product of God's common grace and is available to McDonald's, the YMCA, the homeless shelter, and the political action committee. Such techniques help people feel they've found a place to belong, supply them with a sense of meaning and purpose, help them develop and grow as individuals, and enable them to serve the larger community. What's not to like?

Some critics of "organized religion" decry this reality, as if real people—who they prefer to call "spiritual"—can live as if they never touch the ground, can survive and thrive without employing this collective social wisdom. But if you're going to form and manage a group for any reason or cause, you have to use such techniques.

Furthermore, the New Testament encourages religious behavior here and there. It prohibits sexual license and other forms of immorality. It extols patience, kindness, and other virtues. It tells believers how to worship aright. It instructs churches to care for one another in their common life. In this respect, the New Testament is realistic. It doesn't pretend that the common rules of morality and social concern don't apply to the church. It understands that groups of people, even if you call them churches, have to behave themselves if they're going to get anything done.

So Christianity, like all religions, is a good thing. Unfortunately for the fans of religion, the Holy Spirit is not as interested in religion as we are and, whenever there is an opportunity, has a way of subverting it.

❧

After the church exploded on the scene, it had to attend to all sorts of religious matters: When and where to meet for prayer? Who was going to buy or bake bread for meetings? Who was going to manage money given to the church? Another problem was how to take care of those who had become dependent on the church's generosity, especially widows.

As in any church, especially a rapidly growing church like the one in Jerusalem, there were missteps. "A complaint by the Hellenists arose against the Hebrews because their widows were being neglected in the daily distribution" (Acts 6:1). Thus early in the church's life we see something that has plagued churches ever since: factions—in this case, Hellenists (i.e., Jews immersed in Greco-Roman culture) and Hebrews (i.e., Jews living in Jewish culture). The minority Hellenists were being neglected, as minorities generally are. But give credit to the apostles, who acknowledged the problem, and another problem as well: they couldn't both preach the gospel and "serve tables," as they put it. Not exactly an example of servant leadership, but at least they came up with a solution: appoint a church committee, give the members titles (deacons), and have them attend to the needs of the widows.

This is the sort of thing that religion has always been good at, and this religious solution apparently solved the dispute. It brought peace and order to the church, filled the cupboards of the widows, and contributed to the social well-being of church and society. We don't hear a complaint from the Hellenist widows again.

The one mistake was that the apostles laid hands on these deacons, which was a sacramental way of signaling that these men were now anointed by the Holy Spirit, given spiritual power and authority in a special way. That's just the thing to upset religion. And it didn't take long for one of the deacons, Stephen, to figure that out.

Early on in his diaconate, Stephen got the idea that he shouldn't spend all his time merely performing his assigned religious duty. He recognized that somehow a grace and power was now with him, and instead of merely being religious, he allowed that grace and power to work through him. He started performing "great wonders and signs among the people" (Acts 6:8).

It was his preaching, though, that got Stephen into trouble. Apparently he not only modeled a religion-transcending life but told people not to be satisfied with mere religion. He was accused of speaking blasphemy against Moses (the great lawgiver) and God: "This man never ceases to speak words against this holy place and the law," the authorities exclaimed, and they noted that Jesus would "change the customs Moses delivered to us" (Acts 6:13–14).

Challenging religion will, more times than not, get you into trouble. And this is what happened to Stephen. He was dragged before an impromptu court, and before you know it, he'd been killed by the mob. When the Holy Spirit gets ahold of people, religion usually has to take a backseat, and religion doesn't like the backseat.

Religious people get nervous if you start suggesting that religion isn't all it's cracked up to be, that there is something more important than religion. Religion, when it becomes the focus, is about bringing order and control. It's about making people nicer, happier, and better citizens. It's the middle ground between unbelief and zeal, a safe place to have God and morality without the holy chaos of the Spirit.

Back in the early sixties, a book was published with the title *The Suburban Captivity of the Churches*. The title is still an apt description of an American Christianity that has often traded faith for religion, the life of the Spirit for a life of safety.

The suburbs are not the problem; this form of social life is not the incarnation of evil, as some critics would have us believe. But the suburbs do tend to shape us (as do the city and rural life).[5] And given that the vast majority of churches in America are located in the suburbs, one can see one unhappy consequence of that shaping.

Take one well-known quality of suburban life: safety. I live in a suburb in the Midwest where the biggest news items in the police blotter in our local paper usually have to do with shoplifting or DUIs or the occasional bicycle theft. Murders, rapes, armed robberies, and the like are few and very far between. Those are the types of things that happen in Chicago, not Glen Ellyn, Illinois. Families escape from the insecurity of city life and move to the suburbs because they are, among other things, a safe place to live. Safe is good.

Safety, though, is not a particularly high value in the Christian lifestyle hierarchy. You won't find it in the list of Christian virtues (as in "keep yourself and your family safe"). But that hasn't stopped it from becoming a characteristic of contemporary Christianity.

The yearning for safety begins when we get tired of dealing with the world on the world's terms. At one conference, I had a chance to hear a number of Christian novelists explain why they began writing Christian romances. A typical story went like this: they wanted to share a reading experience with their daughters, so they picked up a few romance novels from Barnes & Noble to read together. But the sub-Christian morality in novel after novel appalled them. Was it not possible to have a romantic story without illicit sex and steamy prose and questionable choices by characters? So they decided to write a Christian romance novel that protected their daughters from such themes.

Or take those who weary of the tired themes of pop music—from silly to raunchy, but seemingly always about romantic love or sex—and so move the radio dial to safe Christian radio. Or those beaten down with the moral pressures they face at work or the untold misery of family dysfunction, who just want Sunday worship to be a sanctuary for one hour per week!

Any Christian who does not get bone tired of dealing with the world on the world's terms has probably lost some basic human sensibility. So there's no denying that we need sanctuaries, safe places to which to retreat—as long as those sanctuaries are also places where we prepare to face danger.

What happens instead is that we begin to conceive of worship, and the entire Christian life, as a sanctuary from the world. We start to limit ourselves to Christian books and Christian music and Christian schools and Christian colleges and Christian movies, so much so that we actually become afraid of the world.

A friend once marveled to me that I let my children attend secular liberal arts colleges; he said he was looking for a Christian college where his daughter could be educated in a safe intellectual environment. My children have regularly run into graduates of Christian schools and colleges who find spending time with non-Christians threatening. While Christian media and education have their place, something has gone seriously wrong with Christians when the world they are called to love and serve, the world for whom Christ died, becomes a place from which they try to protect themselves.

Deacon Stephen wanted nothing of this sort of religion. In his one recorded speech, he criticized the Jews not just for faithlessness toward God but also for their infatuation with religion (in this case religious buildings). In his conclusion, he proclaimed, "The Most High does not dwell in houses made by hands, as the prophet says, 'Heaven is my throne, and the earth is my footstool. What kind of house will you build for me, says the Lord, or what is the place of my rest? Did not my hand make all these things?' " (Acts 7:48–50).

This was not a religious sermon. It did not attempt to make people nice or to bring peace and order to troubled souls. It did not suggest ways for people to become socially useful to the Roman Empire. It did not contain five ways to improve marriages or raise kids. It did not try to help people get control of their moral or spiritual lives. It simply announced the dynamic work of God in history, described how people time and time again resisted that work, and, worst of all, proclaimed that the troublemaker Jesus, who was crucified for crimes against the state and religion, is actually "the Righteous One" (Acts 7:52).

In all this, Stephen stood in a long tradition of prophets, like Isaiah, who denounced mere religion. As we read the New Testament, we are reminded time and again that the gospel isn't about making life safe and orderly, but entails the risk of following Jesus. It's not about improving people, but about killing them and then creating them anew. It's not about helping people make space for spirituality in their busy lives, but about a God who would obliterate our private space and fill it with himself. The gospel is not about getting people to cooperate with God in making the world a better place—to give it a fresh coat of paint, to remodel it. Instead it announces God's plan to raze the present world order and build something new.

When it came to religion, the apostle Paul had no patience. To the church at Colossae, which had a special hankering to be religious rather than Christian, he wrote:

> Let no one pass judgment on you in questions of food and drink, or with regard to a festival or a new moon or a Sabbath. These are a shadow of the things to come, but the substance belongs to Christ. Let no one disqualify you, insisting on asceticism and worship of angels, going on in detail about visions, puffed up without reason by his sensuous mind. . . .

30

If with Christ you died to the elemental spirits of the world, why, as if you were still alive in the world, do you submit to regulations—"Do not handle, Do not taste, Do not touch" (referring to things that all perish as they are used)—according to human precepts and teachings? These have indeed an appearance of wisdom in promoting self-made religion and asceticism and severity to the body, but they are of no value in stopping the indulgence of the flesh. (Col. 2:16–18, 20–23)

Paul says that not only does this sort of thing actually make the moral life harder, it fails to grasp what the Holy Spirit is doing in and through us. The Spirit is not trying to make us more useful church members or better citizens but trying to get us first to see that we're dead—utterly incapable of improvement—and that it's only when we're dead that we have any hope:

If then you have been raised with Christ, seek the things that are above, where Christ is, seated at the right hand of God. Set your minds on things that are above, not on things that are on earth. For you have died, and your life is hidden with Christ in God. When Christ who is your life appears, then you also will appear with him in glory. (Col. 3:1–4)

In short, the New Testament teaches that this world, and every life in it, is a catastrophe, beyond tinkering, beyond remodeling. The gospel is about the cross, which puts a nail in the coffin of religion. The gospel is also about resurrection—not an improvement nor an adjustment, but the breaking in of a completely new life, because the old life has been obliterated. It's about the Holy Spirit introducing holy chaos—the toppling of religion that has become an idol—so that people can know liberation.

It's not just the message but also the means that the Holy Spirit uses to upset religious order. Take the Bible. Before giving us the Bible, God should have attached a warning label: "Danger: Do not use this without proper supervision; handling this could be injurious to spiritual health."

Instead God just gives us the Bible. We take this pack of dynamite (with the fuse lit, no less) and constantly misinterpret and misuse it; we manipulate it to manipulate others and then ignore it when it doesn't suit our purposes. It is supposed to be a means of the gracious revelation of the love of God, but so often we turn it into a new rulebook for the righteous. Yet the Bible's message has a way of breaking through our manipulations and commentaries, our appeals to context or intricate word studies that attempt to dodge the plain sense of the text. It is indeed sharper than a two-edged sword, and it is constantly killing that it may bring to life.

Or take worship, which takes place in a "sanctuary," a safe place. Our services are crowded with cheerful tunes and inspiring sermons, with jokes from the platform and smiles everywhere—so much so that we forget sometimes that we are in the presence of God Almighty, our Maker and Judge and Redeemer. If we drive the Holy Spirit from worship by making it an occasion for mere religious edification, we forget what a dangerous place worship is. As writer Annie Dillard put it in her book *Teaching a Stone to Talk*:

> On the whole, I do not find Christians, outside of the catacombs, sufficiently sensible of conditions. Does anyone have the foggiest idea what sort of power we so blithely invoke? Or, as I suspect, does no one believe a word of it? The churches are children playing on the floor with their chemistry sets, mixing up a batch of TNT to kill a Sunday morning. It is madness to wear ladies' straw hats and velvet hats to church; we should all be wearing crash helmets. Ushers should issue life preservers and signal flares; they should lash us to our pews. For the sleeping god may wake someday and take offense, or the waking god may draw us out to where we can never return.[6]

The problem—our temptation to make Christianity a religion of order and safety—begins with our failure to grasp who Jesus Christ is and how, in the Holy Spirit, he continues to speak and work among us. Dorothy Sayers put it this way:

We have very efficiently pared the claws of the Lion of Judah, certified him "meek and mild," and recommended him as a fitting household pet for pale curates and pious old ladies. To those who knew him, however, he in no way suggests a milk-and-water person; they objected to him as a dangerous firebrand.[7]

Why God would entrust the church with these risky means of grace—worship, the Bible, preaching, and so forth—calling us to speak of the dangerous mercy of his firebrand Son through the mysterious power of the Spirit, I have no idea. But this God seems addicted to risk rather than religion, to freedom rather than control, to love rather than law. In entrusting the future of the planet to a mercurial nomad named Abraham; in revealing his holy will to a fickle and forgetful people; in coming in the flesh to make things plain to the blind and deaf, who wanted nothing more than to murder him—this God seems oblivious to the dangers that accompany his unmerited favor.

And then he has the nerve to tell us to imitate him (see Eph. 5:1). This is not the type of person into whose hands most people would entrust the leadership of their church. Well, except in an honorary capacity.

In the second half of this book, I will suggest the various and sundry ways we let religion—addiction to order and control in the name of God—get the better of us. But before we go there, we need to see more clearly the life God calls us into. And to do that, we need to spend a little time unpacking one dimension of the biblical narrative that seems forgotten in our day.

2

THE EUCATASTROPHE

Once upon a time before time, "God created the heavens and the earth. The earth was without form and void, and darkness was over the face of the deep" (Gen. 1:1–2). Thus writes the author of the book of Genesis. The account, now thousands of years old, still elicits no small amount of scientific and historical controversy. But first and foremost, it is a God-breathed *story*, a story with its own logic.

Scholars debate the exact meaning of the opening line—is it a thesis for what follows? Or is it the first act of creation? A simple reading seems best: God has created in rudimentary form the sky and the earth. But the earth was "without form": that is, it didn't have any land; there were no mountains or valleys, no canyons or deserts. No shapes or form. No property with a view.[1]

It was also "void"—of plants, animals, and people. No roses or thorn trees. No eagles or mosquitos; no giraffes or black widow spiders. No pesky neighbors with barking dogs or beautiful people to admire.

Not that one could have seen anything anyway, for the narrative says there was darkness everywhere.

And water was ubiquitous. No oceanfront property. Just ocean. No tides or waves—because there was no moon to pull the water to and fro. The water that covered the earth is pictured as a placid lake at dawn.

Except that there was no dawn, no rising sun, no rooster crowing, no sparrows chirping to welcome the new day. Just darkness, and silence in the darkness. Not a scary darkness or unnerving silence—for there was nothing yet to be scared of. No, no, quite the opposite. This darkness and silence made for utter calm, like the peace of a deep, restful sleep.

So, in the very beginning there was complete order and tranquility.

The author of this book says the Spirit of God brooded over this order and tranquility—and then began to tinker.

The first thing he did was to create light. So now there was darkness *and* light. The creation had become dynamic. Light and darkness opposed one another. So different were they, they were given separate names: "day" and "night." And this was only the beginning, day one.

Next God made sky, and so a new dynamic was introduced. Now there was "the waters" and "the heavens."

The next day land was formed, with a new dynamic still: "seas" and "earth." Now there was night and day, sky and waters, earth and sea. God was up to something.

In the middle of the third day, God really got going. He created plants and trees and all manner of vegetation. Chrysanthemums bursting with color, stately redwoods stretching to the heavens, and prairie grass waving elegantly in the wind. And, we must assume, poison oak and thornbushes and deadly mushrooms. And he gave this resplendent variety of plants and trees the ability to reproduce, to be fruitful and multiply by propagating their own seeds. As we know, this ability tends to wildness—the lush and verdant chaos of life.

Having caused enough trouble in three days, God took his mind off the earth for a bit. He started tinkering with the gift wrapping, that which enveloped this planet. He created the sun, a bright and warm thing that penetrated deeply into the skin of the planet. Then by way of contrast came the moon—a beautiful but distant orb that hung in the sky like a shiny earring. And then came the bow on the wrapping: stars. Billions of them. This was variety gone to seed, variety without number, a metaphysical chaos of the heavens.

That was already quite a day's work, but unfazed, God turned his attention back to this planet and really set things on edge. Vegetation is resplendent enough, but any plant or tree is pretty much stuck in place, confined to living in one spot its whole life. But what if there could be a form of life that could move around on the face of the planet, that could crawl or run or jump or fly?

And what if these mobile creatures didn't merely exist side by side but interacted with one another? What if they absolutely depended on one another, needed each other to live, so that there was a paradoxical dynamic in which living creatures had to both pursue and be pursued, devour and be devoured by their fellow creatures in order for life to continue to explode on the planet?

So God created living creatures, swarms of them. Creatures in the ocean. Creatures on the land. Creatures in the skies. Creatures, creatures everywhere—trout and sharks, deer and wolves, robins and vultures, among others. And the number of living creatures—if you include the insects, which of course we must—would be millions upon millions. As with the plants, he gave these creatures the ability to self-propagate. And just to make himself clear, God said to the creatures, "Be fruitful and multiply." As if instinct would not have taken over soon enough.

The planet was now one fine mess. From a state of perfect peace and harmony, it had been transformed in a few short days into a lush, rich, infinitely varied cacophony of color and sound and life.

This is the sort of thing that happens when the Spirit of God tinkers.

And God wasn't done. A workweek of activity had left the planet in a state of holy confusion. But God decided to work the weekend, at least the first day of the weekend. He had one more idea to put on the table before he took a break. And what he did next suggests that one should not push it, that one's best ideas are not necessarily those that come at the end of a hard week. But God went ahead anyway, oblivious to the consequences.

He created people. And he created them in his image and likeness: Mischief makers. Creatures who cannot leave well enough alone. Creatures like animals, restless and on the move. Creatures who pursue and are pursued. Creatures never satisfied with the status quo, with the way things are, born to create something new again and again. Creatures who want to plan and build and paint and carve and hunt and fish and play—and who knows what else?

And if that were not enough, he created people in two varieties, male and female. Of the same flesh and blood, to be sure, but as different as night is from day, as the seas are from sky, as the waters are from the land. Of the same being and substance, but as different as Mars is from Venus. This is not a combination easy to explain.

And here comes a most mysterious thing. To the man and the woman he gave the wild and unruly gift of sex. And without a warning label. Without instructions. Well, except this one: "Be fruitful and multiply." Have lots and lots of unprotected sex. Not exactly responsible family planning. No concerns about the woman's career or the man's freedom.

No precise formula of 1.8 children. No issues with carbon footprints or affordability or the ability to spend quality time with each child. Just the command to create little communities of chaos and love called families.

The Spirit of God—the Mischief Maker—was now finally through. The calm, orderly, and peaceful creation—peaceful as a deep sleep, orderly and calm as a placid lake at dawn—had been turned into a variety of form, a chaos of color and sound. The eucatastrophe, the good catastrophe, of life was exploding in all corners, spewing forth the volcanic heat and energy of creativity and love and new life. If the Spirit had been brooding when he started, he must have been smiling by the end of day six. He could finally rest, knowing he'd set the world on a course from which it would never recover.

In Genesis, this story is told again, from another angle, but the point seems to be the same: a profusion of form and life that knows no boundary or order. The man is told to name every beast of the field and bird of the heavens, a task we're still feverishly trying to complete. One imagines that the Mischief Maker gave us this job as a practical joke, to point out that it was an impossible job, so resplendent was the creation.

Another practical joke seems to have been the command to work and keep the garden. Work it, yes. Keep it—well, gardens are unruly things. They start off well enough, with neat borders framing orderly rows of seeds or seedlings. It isn't long before unwelcome guests, "weeds," are crowding in, and not long before the seedlings are pushing each other around and then spilling over the neat rows and borders. And then all those uninvited pests trying to feed themselves, swarming over everything, chewing away here and there. Make no mistake: to garden is to war, to battle with life itself, which comes at you like an invading army. Forget to pay attention for just a few days, and the enemy overwhelms you with superior forces, and the garden becomes a jungle.

What makes the man's task even more impossible is that he is not given a little plot to manage, like some small corner of a backyard. This would have been hard enough. But his garden seems to be, well, everywhere—"dominion over . . . all the earth," as Genesis puts it (1:26). Work and keep *everything*.

No wonder the man needs a helpmate. But we'll see, as the story unfolds, that even that won't do the trick. One suspects that this may be one thing that prompted the woman to decide that enough was enough.

3

ANOTHER EUCATASTROPHE

The man and woman together were "keeping" the garden—that impossible but joy-filled task set before them. I imagine them as children on a merry-go-round, spinning faster and faster, trying to shout to the one spinning them, "Stop!" but laughing so hard they couldn't get the word out. The fulsomeness of life sprung up all around them, its variety and chaos always on the verge of overwhelming them. But when they just let it be and did freely what they were commanded—to till and keep the merry-go-round of life—all was well.

There was one thing they were commanded *not* to do: while delighting in the fruit that this cornucopia supplied them, they were told by God not to eat the fruit of one tree, the one called the tree of the knowledge of good and evil (see Gen. 2:16–17).[1]

Though the story contains no philosophical discourse on the nature of *good* and *evil*, much of the character of these two words is strongly implied. The man and the woman were experiencing the good—this was nothing less than the life that had been handed them on a garden platter, that cacophony of meaningful labor and exorbitant life and joy.

The man and the woman knew something of ethics. They were commanded to do good: Be fruitful and multiply. Name the animals. Cling to one another. Tend the garden. By implication, they could surmise what evil might be: to refuse to be fruitful, to neglect the naming of animals, to wander from one another, to let the garden go willy-nilly.

So in Genesis 3 the man and woman already have some knowledge of good and evil. Combine that with natural human curiosity, and you've got trouble. The narrator of Genesis could have pictured the next event as the internal wrestling of the human mind—the sort of mental wrestling we well recognize today. Instead he describes it as a conversation between a crafty serpent and the naïve but well-meaning woman.

The serpent begins with the suggestion that is more or less true, something a curious person would have begun to wonder anyway: "Did God actually say, 'You shall not eat of any tree in the garden'?" (3:1). It's a question that makes sense if one is exhausted, perhaps at the end of another hectic day of trying to rein in the exploding chaos of the garden. It's the type of exaggeration—what psychologists call "globalizing"—that you are tempted toward when you're at the end of your rope. You look at the one thing you cannot have, and you say, "Every tree in the garden might as well be off limits if I can't have the one I desire!" It's petulant, but not surprising.

The woman is sensible enough to recall, "We may eat of the fruit of the trees in the garden, but God said, 'You shall not eat of the fruit of the tree that is in the midst of the garden, neither shall you touch it, lest you die'" (3:2–3).

It does not appear that death in any form has entered the picture, so it would have been an unimaginable concept. It's difficult to grasp the nature of an event you have never witnessed. It's another boundary not to be crossed, yes, but another idea about which human curiosity—a good and blessed thing—would naturally wonder.

Then comes the line that turns the conversation south: "You will not surely die. For God knows that when you eat of it your eyes will be opened, and you will be like God, knowing good and evil" (3:4–5).

A series of assumptions seems to drive this speech, and all of them prove to be true, especially in view of the entire biblical narrative.

The man and the woman do not die after eating of the tree. And though some years later they return to dust (see Gen. 3:19), the whole arc of the Bible suggests that this death is hardly the last word. God's intention for them from beginning to end was life eternal with him.

The eyes of the man and the woman are indeed opened. As a result of taking from this tree, they gain a deeper and wider knowledge of good and evil. This is something that complicates their lives terribly, alternatively ennobling them and enslaving them, but something that in fact begins to mature them.

The man and the woman—and especially their descendants—have been set on a path to become like God. To become "partakers of the divine nature" (2 Peter 1:4) is in fact the *telos*, the biblical goal of God for humanity.

The woman is not only curious but practical—another virtuous human trait. She sees that "the tree was good for food." The man and the woman had already experienced that connection in many ways. You cannot put a glass of water before a thirsty man and expect him not to grab it and drink. You cannot give the man and the woman sexual desire and a pleasing partner and not expect them to make love. And one can hardly set before the man and the woman a tree bearing luscious fruit and not expect them to partake.

The woman sees that the tree is "a delight to the eyes." It is beautiful. Again, we see a noble human virtue—the ability to recognize and appreciate the beauty of God's creation—rising to the surface. We are naturally drawn to beauty. We not only want to behold it but also want to touch it, to be a part of it and for it to be a part of us.

Finally, the woman recognizes that this mythical tree can make her wise. Once more, we see a noble human virtue—the yearning for wisdom. And the man and the woman are in desperate need of wisdom. They have a relationship to negotiate, and eventually offspring to raise, and animals to name, and a garden exploding with life and unimaginable energy to manage. The woman is to be commended for recognizing that she doesn't have it all together, that she needs help, that she and her man need guidance if they are going to exercise dominion.

So she reaches out, grabs a piece of fruit, and sinks her teeth into it. She calls to the man, "Honey, come try some of this."

Immediately they know something is amiss. Their eyes have been opened, all right. They have quickly become smarter and wiser. They recognize, for example, how vulnerable they were, how exposed they are to the elements and to one another, how their sexuality is not only a sign of their unity but now also of their disunity. It hints that a thing designed for mutual love might now also be a source of power and deception and exploitation.

They also recognize that their relationship with their Creator has changed. Again, they show noble instincts: they experience a proper sense of guilt and shame. They know better than to imagine that they've done nothing wrong. They are sensible enough to recognize that something is broken in their relationship with God. They instinctively know that to stand before him boldly as if nothing has happened would be a farce.

When confronted by their Creator, they play the blame game—the man blames the woman, and the woman the serpent. God seems to go along, which suggests that it is not merely a game. The three are not equally guilty. The guilt of the man and the woman is of a different order than the guilt of the serpent, and it is to the serpent that God turns first and most decisively.

Simply put, the serpent is damned: "Cursed are you," says the Lord God (3:14). God also judges the man and the woman shortly thereafter. But the tempter's judgment seems without hope.

To be sure, there are serious consequences for the woman and the man. But the consequences are not due merely to "willful rebellion," some powerful and prideful obstinance. Nothing in this story suggests something so strong. Here weakness is mixed with pride, curiosity with naïveté, and righteous longing with disobedience. The original sin described here is not the raising of the angry fist before God, as much as it is stupidity and immaturity. And impatience. For all that the woman longs for in taking the fruit is something that God intends to give them in his good time and in his way. The original sin of the man and woman is indeed a form of pride, and more than anything, it is a desire to control the timing and process of their growth and maturity in God. The consequences that God metes out seem to accord with the nature of the crime.

For example, for the woman, bearing children will be more painful than ever. It's not as if pain was not to be a part of childbearing from the beginning. The only difference now is that it is "multiplied." In addition, it's not merely physical pain that is in view. It is surely that, but physical pain becomes a negative sacrament of the suffering involved in bringing children into the world. Now the woman will know a deeper ambiguity and heartache, along with joy and pride, in bearing and raising children—of seeing them struggle as they grow and mature, of wistfully watching them leave mother and father and cling to new mates.

The woman will now also be subjected to a tension she will never be able to escape. She will yearn to be ever more intimate with her husband, but that very intimacy will feel confining to her. She will spend her days negotiating a compulsive longing for her husband and a desire for freedom—both innate and good human longings that only with wisdom and maturity will finally be seen as one and the same.

But it also means something more dreary: a relationship characterized by freedom and companionship—as helpmates one to another—now would become an oppressive hierarchy. And the oppressiveness of that most intimate of relationships would become the norm, and not just in marriage but in other spheres as well. As Aristotle was to put it later, "So it is naturally with the male and the female; the one is superior, the other inferior; the one governs, the other is governed; and the same rule must necessarily hold good with respect to all mankind."[2]

To the man God said, "Cursed is the ground because of you" (3:17). Again note the graciousness of God: not the man but the ground is cursed. That which was to be a source of meaning and purpose—the tilling and keeping of the garden—now becomes a burden. The pleasure of labor is not removed, but now added to it is a measure of ambiguity that will plague man. "By the sweat of your face you shall eat bread," said God (3:19). That which was designed to bring the man joy would also become that which he will dread. Life will no longer be lived merely in joy and freedom but also in dreary predictability. It was now characterized not only as *work* but also as *toil*, with the frustration that implies. At times it will all seem futile, for the earth that we cultivate for life now also becomes a symbol of our death: to dust we shall return. Not a happy picture.

This ambiguity is never expressed better than in the words of a later poet:

> Vanity of vanities, says the Preacher,
> vanity of vanities! All is vanity.
> What does man gain by all the toil
> at which he toils under the sun?

A generation goes, and a generation comes,
  but the earth remains forever.
The sun rises, and the sun goes down,
  and hastens to the place where it rises.
The wind blows to the south
  and goes around to the north;
around and around goes the wind,
  and on its circuits the wind returns.
All streams run to the sea,
  but the sea is not full;
to the place where the streams flow,
  there they flow again.
All things are full of weariness;
  a man cannot utter it. (Eccles. 1:2–8)

What makes a poem like this so full of pathos is the reality that always exists alongside it, which the psalmist expresses with equal eloquence:

O Lord, our Lord . . .
what is man that you are mindful of him,
  and the son of man that you care for him?
Yet you have made him a little lower than the heavenly beings
  and crowned him with glory and honor.
You have given him dominion over the works of your
  hands;
  you have put all things under his feet. (Ps. 8:1, 4–6)

The fate of the man and the woman is to live in the knowledge of both glory *and* curse, good *and* evil, life *and* death—side by side, even woven together, forever. Well, not quite forever. For God in his goodness will not countenance a full-scale disaster.

First, he protects their vulnerability, before the world and before each other: he clothes them in something more durable and beautiful than the paltry fig leaves they had fashioned. By implication, he sacrifices the life of some of his own good

46

creatures to do this. This hints that God is willing to go to extraordinary lengths—even the death of the good—to care for his human creation.

Second, he drives them from the garden, lest the man "reach out his hand and take also of the tree of life and eat, and live forever" (Gen. 3:22). At first this seems like another punishment—to be banned from the blessed garden. But in fact it is a blessing to be banned. To live forever in the ambiguity of good and evil, of life and death, of hope and despair— an existence without resolution or hope of resolution—this would be a curse worse than death. So God drives them from this existence and makes sure that they will never be able to enter it, at least until all is ready.

Third, as the larger biblical story unfolds, we see that the so-called curses we now live under will in fact become blessings. All that oppresses humankind and tempts us to despair—"poverty of spirit"—will become the road to liberation. All that causes grief and lament—"mourning"—will become a source of deep comfort. All human longings that frustrate us because they seem incapable of fulfillment— "hungering and thirsting for righteousness"—will become a sign of their ultimate fulfillment.[3]

It would appear then that God has now permitted another level of chaos to enter the created order, chaos characterized by suffering and death. But this chaos, like the chaos of the original creation and the chaos of the new creation we'll see at Pentecost, is just another means of bringing men and women into full freedom as his children.

4

CONTROL ADDICTION

Though they have been spared unrelenting suffering, from this day forward the man and woman—now called Adam and Eve—and all their descendants live under another type of curse.

It is an addiction that becomes manifest immediately. Eve bears two sons, Cain and Abel (see Gen. 4). Cain is like his father, a farmer, and Abel branches out and becomes a herdsman. They are both devout, and as apparently is their custom, one day they bring to God thank offerings, the firstfruits of their labors. It is unclear how he comes to perceive this, but Cain grasps that Abel's offering is pleasing to God while his is not.

Cain's face falls, and anger boils within him. The Genesis story doesn't explain but merely assumes sibling rivalry. It is not hard to imagine Cain thinking, *I've worked as hard as my brother, and I am no less devout! What's going on?*

No explanation is forthcoming from God. Only some advice about Cain not letting anger get the best of him. "Stay the course," God essentially says, "and in good time, your offering too will be accepted."

But it appears that Cain is not interested in waiting in good time—a very similar impatience to that of his mother and father. One can imagine that God's refusal to explain himself, and what seemed his tyrannizing morality, infuriates Cain, as it has so many people since.

Cain, apparently in the haze and heat of bitterness, strikes at the symbol of his impotence: he kills his brother. It is not an act that proceeds from cold logic. If asked if he did it to push God into a corner, to make God accept his offering, to force God's hand, Cain would likely have laughed at the absurdity (as we do in such situations). But years later, after maturing, he may have just as likely nodded knowingly.

In any event, God announces more consequences (exile for Cain, and the ground is cursed not only with sweat but also with blood) and more grace (Cain will be spared the death penalty). But the pattern set when Eve bit into the fruit has taken on flesh in the next generation.

And in the next. And in the next. Story after story in Genesis repeats the same story, relives the same curse, in which people succumb over and over to the same addiction. God will attempt to lead his lost people into new lush places, but he will have to both judge and forgive time and again.

Take the story of the Shinarites, better known as the Tower of Babel, in Genesis 11. The story is set in a time when the whole earth shared the same language, used the same words to mean the same things. The people had just made their way east and had settled in a plain called Shinar. They were builders, and ambitious builders at that.

"Come," they prod one another, "let us build ourselves a city and a tower with its top in the heavens, and let us make a name for ourselves, lest we be dispersed over the face of the whole earth" (v. 4).

As the story unfolds, it's apparent that God is not pleased with the Shinarites. The assumption of many hearers of this story is that the problem is pride. The Shinarites want to build a tower to heaven, a magnificent architectural structure that rivals God himself. And they want to make a name for themselves—do themselves proud.

It's at this point that I believe many commentators go awry. Other stories in Genesis suggest that God is not threatened when people use their ingenuity and courage to build great things, like the ark of the covenant, the temple, and the city of David. The greatness of humankind is not a temptation but a cause for praise: "What is man that you are mindful of him?" as we've noted the psalmist said. "You have made him a little lower than the heavenly beings. . . . You have given him dominion over the works of your hands" (Ps. 8:4–6).

Neither does the desire to have a great name and good reputation seem to be a cause for concern. God himself soon will tell Abram that "I will make of you a great nation, and I will bless you and make your name great" (Gen. 12:2).

In their desire to build something magnificent, the people of Shinar are doing nothing more than fulfilling their divine calling to have dominion over the whole earth, including the architectural arts.

No, the phrase that stuck in God's craw, I believe, was not the desire to do something worthy of those made in God's image. It was when the Shinarites said, "lest we be dispersed over the face of the whole earth" (Gen. 11:4).

The Shinarites sought to cement the order and uniformity of their life together. They were a growing people, apparently, and they longed to hold on to what they had. They did not so much want to be fruitful and multiply and spread over the face of the earth as much as stay small and confined to what they already knew.

"Behold, they are one people," ponders God when he hears their plans, "and they have all one language, and this is only the beginning of what they will do. And nothing that they propose to do will now be impossible for them" (Gen. 11:6).

Again, we are tempted to interpret this as if God is threatened by their success. But instead it signals God's compassion. As later history reveals, when there is no inherent brake on such desires, communities become not islands of freedom and love but cesspools of social uniformity. On the one hand, the righteous desire for community and order can become utopian, a yearning that visionaries ever since have tried to incarnate by any means possible. When the yearning for community becomes a premature desire for utopia, what we produce is dystopia: oppressive, despotic, cultic, authoritarian communities. The desire of the Shinarites is the desire that would later captivate the hearts of Lenin and Hitler—of anyone who yearns for a perfect social order and uniformity of culture, who pines after racial and social purity. If you give such people a little bit of rope, they'll hang their neighbors and eventually themselves in the process.

God sees disaster coming to Shinar, and he takes drastic but merciful steps. He creates an explosion of language. He unleashes communication chaos, social chaos that forces people to multiply in new ways. Thus, people are driven to gather in like-language groups, and from there they go off to create unique and separate cultures; they disperse "over the face of all the earth" (Gen. 11:9). The way this story has it, in one fell swoop, God creates global multiculturalism—a cacophony of people, customs, habits, languages, music—the splendid chaos of pluralism.

This story will continue to unfold all through the Old Testament. The prophet Micah will see a vision of the future Zion, the center of God's capital: the "peoples" will flow to it, the "nations" shall come, in wondrous variety, not to become a single political order, let alone a unified religious order: "For all the peoples," he writes, "walk each in the name of its god" (Mic. 4:5)—each with their own language, customs, and culture. They will not even share possessions, a common symbol of human unity, but each will sit under his own vine and his own fig tree—all in blessed variety (see Mic. 4:1–5).

We see the same at the end of the Bible. Regarding God's future capital, the new Jerusalem, the writer says, "By its light will the nations walk, and the kings of the earth will bring their glory into it" (Rev. 21:24). Again, there is a divine relishing of the cultural achievements of humankind: the kings will bring *their* glory, that is, the glory of their unique and individual political and cultural achievements.

But even before that, note what is now called the story of Pentecost (see Acts 2). Many commentators note how this event supposedly *reverses* the judgment on the people of Shinar, where language was confused and people were separated. At Pentecost understanding is returned and people are united. Yes and no. At Pentecost it is not that everyone again speaks the same language. No, instead each hears about the wonderful works of God *in his own language*! The beautiful cacophony of human language, and therefore culture, is retained.

In one sense, the story of Shinar is indeed a story of divine judgment against human addiction to order. In another, though, it is an ironic extension of the divine command to "be fruitful and multiply" and the Spirit of God's relentless drive to push his creation to the edge of chaos. It is not the last time that one divine action cuts two ways.

THE ORDEAL AND THE PROMISE

"Go from your country and your kindred and your father's house to the land that I will show you," God tells a man named Abram, who had been living in a land called Ur (modern Iraq). "And I will make of you a great nation, and I will bless you and make your name great, so that you will be a blessing" (Gen. 12:1–2). Thus begins the next chapter in the ongoing saga of humankind's addiction to order and control—and of the divine response of judgment and mercy.

"So Abram went, as the LORD had told him," writes the Genesis author (12:4). He and his wife, Sarai; his nephew, Lot; and a host of others leave their home and journey far away, to the land that God indeed shows them—Canaan. When they arrive at a place called Shechem, the Lord appears to Abram, and as if to put an exclamation point on it, repeats the promise: "To your offspring I will give this land" (12:7).

At that time, Canaanites and other ethnic groups inhabited the land. It was not yet Abram's land to have and to hold.

But Abram seems grateful for the promise, and he builds an altar at Shechem. He next goes to a place called Bethel, and there he builds another altar, seemingly for the same purpose.

Then in the land of divine promise, a famine arises. Not only have the Canaanites not departed, but it no longer seems to be a land one could support a family on. Maybe this wasn't the particular land that God had promised. Maybe Abram had misheard. Maybe it had been nothing but a dream. For it is difficult to believe that *this land*, the land with no prospects, the land filled with people who know not the true God, is to be Abram's. Since it is not working out as he had thought, Abram takes the bull by the horns. He has a family to feed, after all.

He moves the family to a place with some prospects, Egypt, where Abram shows himself to be both a crafty businessman and a wicked husband to the woman through whom God had promised to bless the world. Abram convinces Sarai to masquerade as his sister. He believes that if Egypt's Pharaoh knew that Sarai was his wife, he would be killed so that Pharaoh could do with Sarai as he pleased. If Sarai was only his "sister," then Pharaoh could still do with her as he pleased with no need to kill her "brother." To be fair to Abram, he may have justified his abominable behavior like this: If he was killed, how could God possibly fulfill his promise through him? Abram is a builder of altars, a devout man. He likely thinks he is helping out God by preventing his own death. He likely reasons, *It isn't as if God can raise people from the dead.*

Whatever Abram's precise motives, Sarai goes along and becomes a state concubine, and that connection to the house of Pharaoh opens doors for Abram. He becomes a man of considerable wealth and, like all men of considerable wealth, considerable influence. *So there you go*, Abram may have thought, *the promise is being fulfilled. My name is great, and with my wealth, I will be a blessing!*

At some point, Pharaoh figures out what was going on and summarily boots Abram and Sarai out of the country.

Still, Abram arrives back at Bethel "very rich in livestock, in silver, and in gold" (Gen. 13:2).

Apparently the land is no longer suffering under a famine, but the Canaanites and others are still entrenched. Add to that the holdings of nephew Lot (who apparently had also done well during this interlude), and perhaps Abram is feeling that he will never have this land to himself. Abram surveys his prospects with a realistic eye. Aside from the Canaanites, he believes the land that remains cannot support both him and Lot ("the land could not support both of them dwelling together; for their possessions were so great that they could not dwell together," says Genesis 13:6). So he cuts a deal with Lot, who heads toward the Jordan Valley.

Just when Abram has successfully manipulated affairs in his favor, God reveals himself again, as if to say that Abram's efforts are in the end pointless. He tells him to look around to the north, south, east, and west—where all Abram can see is Canaanites and Perizzites and Lot's family—and says, "All the land that you see I will give to you and to your offspring" (Gen. 13:15).

There is that word again, *offspring*. The parts of the promise—the land, the great name—are slowly taking shape. But there is no sign of the offspring. Though Abram can manipulate some things, this business of offspring is completely out of his control.

Local politics and warfare distract Abram for a while, but when things settle down, it appears that the issue of an heir has been weighing on him. In Genesis 15 the Lord appears to Abram in a vision and reassures him, but Abram presses the point: "O Lord GOD, what will you give me, for I continue childless. . . . You have given me no offspring." Abram points to Eliezer of Damascus, a member of his clan but hardly his own son, saying, "A member of my household will be my heir" (vv. 2–3).

The Lord again reassures him, "This man shall not be your heir; your very own son shall be your heir" (v. 4).

Then God gives Abram another and even more dramatic object lesson. Abram should look not just horizontally, but up: "Look toward heaven, and number the stars, if you are able to number them. . . . So shall your offspring be" (v. 5).

Genesis says, "And he believed the LORD" (v. 6). But ensuing events suggest it is a faith still mixed with doubt.

The conversation continues in the months and years following. When later the Lord promises Abram once more that he will indeed possess the land, Abram wavers, asking, "How am I to know that I shall possess it?" (Gen. 15:8).

What happens next is one of the more unusual mystical experiences recorded in the history of spirituality (see Gen. 15:9–21). It suggests that Abram was wrestling mightily with the divine promise.

Abram hears God tell him to prepare a sacrifice, but vultures descend on the carcasses Abram had slaughtered in preparation. Abram drives them away, and the sacrifice is apparently aborted. Abram then falls into a deep sleep, during which a "dreadful and great darkness fell upon him" (v. 12). He dreams that God speaks to him, telling him of terrible events to unfold, in which his heirs will be enslaved in a foreign land for four centuries. God tells him that his own life will end in peace and that his heirs will eventually be liberated and return to Canaan, but the dream ends with the mysterious and troubling saying: "And they shall come back here in the fourth generation, for the iniquity of the Amorites is not yet complete" (v. 16)—as if to portend more troubles for his descendants.

In the middle of the night—or maybe it is the next night (it's unclear whether all this occurs in one night or over two days)—Abram has a vision of a smoking pot and a flaming torch, and he hears once again the divine promise, but this time it encompasses a land mass much greater than Canaan, extending from Egypt to Mesopotamia.

This incident was no doubt as terrifying and comforting to Abram as it is enigmatic to us today. If any of this assures Abram, it does nothing to assuage Sarai, who soon afterward tells Abram that it's time to take matters into their own hands (see Gen. 16).

"The LORD has prevented me from bearing children," she tells her husband. "Go in to my servant; it may be that I shall obtain children by her" (v. 2). That Abram—despite the repeated visions, despite his protestation of faith—submits to Sarai's request without an argument ("And Abram listened to the voice of Sarai," v. 2), suggests that Abram agreed that if this offspring was to happen, Abram had to become the master of his fate.

As one might expect, the situation blew up in their faces. To make a long story short, Hagar, the servant, did indeed conceive a child, which only prompted her to look with contempt upon the barren Sarai. Sarai, ashamed and bitter, drove Hagar from the home. Eventually Hagar rejoins the household and gives birth to Ishmael, but as the story later shows, things were never the same.

Again—how many times has it been now?—the Lord promises to give Abram and Sarai not only a child but offspring in spades. It would seem that the longer the promise is delayed and the more doubts Abram and Sarai have, the more the promise grows. Abraham—a new name now given him—will be "the father of a multitude of nations" (Gen. 17:3). As if Abraham didn't get this, the Lord repeats, "I have made you the father of a multitude of nations," and then adds for emphasis, "I will make you exceedingly fruitful, and I will make you into nations, and kings shall come from you" (Gen. 17:5–6). It is the lush, overflowing, chaotic garden applied specifically to Abraham's offspring. His family will be rich in numbers, in variety, in power, in influence. And he will be given a lush garden of his own—"all the land of Canaan, for an everlasting possession, and I will be their God" (Gen. 17:8).

And a new promise!—"and I will be their God." It's not just a promise to do something *for* Abraham, but a promise to do something *with* Abraham and his descendants. "I will establish my covenant between me and you and your offspring after you throughout their generations of an everlasting covenant, to be God to you and to your offspring" (Gen. 17:7). The promise is also about an everlasting relationship.

God then gets specific. Sarah (who is also given a name change) will conceive. Not Hagar or any other servant, but Sarah.

It's at this point that Abraham turns bitter. He's heard the promise for decades and nothing has come of it. Now he is an old man, beyond his ability to impregnate a woman. Similarly Sarah, for whom menopause is a distant memory. When Abraham hears the promise this time, he falls on the ground and laughs. He chuckles cynically about his and Sarah's chances of having a child at their advanced ages. Having abandoned all hope, he reminds God of the only realistic possibility now: "Oh that Ishmael might live before you!" (Gen. 17:18).

A later biblical writer noted that the mercy of the Lord is from everlasting to everlasting, and this may have been one incident he had in mind. Amazingly, the Lord does not become impatient or angry or strike Abraham for his lack of faith. He just calmly repeats himself, "No, but Sarah your wife shall bear you a son, and you shall call his name Isaac" (Gen. 17:19). God seems to have the patience of a saint.

A little while later, it is Sarah who laughs in despair when the promise is repeated again. This time, God's patience seems to be tested, for he replies, "Is anything too hard for the LORD?" (Gen. 18:14).

The answer comes within a year: "The LORD visited Sarah as he had said," says Genesis, "and the LORD did to Sarah as he had promised" (21:1). The child is named Isaac, as instructed, and circumcised to fulfill Abraham's part in the covenant. Their despair turns into joy: "God has made laughter for me," cries Sarah; "everyone who hears will laugh over me" (21:6).

And she marvels: "Who would have said to Abraham that Sarah would nurse children? Yet I have borne him a son in his old age" (21:7). It is all too good to be true.

Still, they do not live happily ever after, even after the miracle. It doesn't clear up family resentments. One day Sarah sees Ishmael laughing. Just the sight of the son of Hagar, an Egyptian, sharing in the joys of her household—the now blessed household, a gifted household, the household of promise—is enough to set Sarah off. She storms up to Abraham and demands, "Cast out this slave woman with her son, for the son of this slave woman shall not be heir with my son Isaac" (Gen. 21:10). Abraham again shows no backbone and relents. He sends Hagar and Ishmael, the product of his loins, into the wilderness of Beersheba with nothing but some bread and a skin of water.

It would not be the last time in history that someone who had received extraordinary blessings would turn that blessing into a curse for others.

And it would not be the last time in history that God would appear to take away that which he had so graciously given. A few years later—Isaac is a boy now—Abraham hears a request that makes today's reader's blood turn cold. It apparently did not make Abraham's blood do so, for nothing in the account as given in Genesis suggests that it bothered Abraham at all.

This is what Abraham hears God say to him: "Take your son, your only son Isaac, whom you love, and go to the land of Moriah, and offer him there as a burnt offering on one of the mountains of which I shall tell you" (Gen. 22:2).

And this is Abraham's response: "So Abraham rose early in the morning" (Gen. 22:3). He asks two servants to assist him. He splits some logs, saddles and loads his donkey, and sets out for Moriah. Abraham asks no questions, expresses no doubt. He does not laugh derisively, nor does he attempt to take matters into his own hands. It is hard to say whether Abraham is in a state of shock or is experiencing mystical madness. Later writers would have us believe that he is acting in profound faith. But it is often difficult to discern the difference between madness and faith.

Later writers will say that Abraham is afraid to lose his son, but the story suggests no fear—no fear of what will happen if he does not do this, and no fear of what will happen if he does. It is Isaac who puts two and two together and haltingly asks what is going on—"Father, where is the lamb for the burnt offering?"—sensing full well what the occasion portends.

To this Abraham implacably responds, "God will provide for himself the lamb for a burnt offering, my son" (Gen. 22:8).

No questions. No doubts. No laughter. Everything that Abraham's life stands for, the very person who represents the meaning of Abraham's existence, the one whose birth makes up for the betrayal of Sarah in Egypt, the lies to Pharaoh, the panicky affair with Hagar, and the cowardice of exiling Hagar and Ishmael—the very justification for Abraham's existence—is on the line. One might suppose that Abraham has finally decided, after failing time and again his entire life, that he is called not to manipulate, not to bring order and meaning to his life by his own wits, not to justify his existence with his own works. The calmness and fortitude with which he goes forth on this macabre ordeal suggests he enjoys a peace that passes understanding, a freedom that only saints and mystics have known. Or, again, maybe it's just madness.

Yet it is at the moment when "madness" takes over completely, when Abraham is about to plunge the knife into the breast of his only son—at the moment when it is absolutely clear that Abraham has forsaken all attempts to control the divine command and promise—that is when the divine command and promise reveals itself for what it is. Abraham, with the knife poised, is told to stop and listen. He hears a ram caught by the horns in a thick bush. He kills it, just as he would have killed his only son. And he pours the blood out on a make-do altar, just as he would have poured out the blood of the son of promise.

He decides he will never forget this moment nor this place. He calls it "The LORD will provide" (Gen. 22:14). The simple name belies the ordeal that preceded it. It has been a pilgrimage dark and impenetrable—in which hope was mixed with despair, free trust mingled with a desire to control, and the threat of death with resurrection.

6

EARLY SIGNS OF LIBERATION

Story after story in the Old Testament tells the same story—
of a God who offers the freedom of obedience to a people
addicted to control. Of a God who wills to provide for his
people, and of a people who just can't believe it even when
the evidence fills their hungry stomachs with heavenly bread.
Of a God who time and again manifests his promise—and
thus offers an invitation to live in trust—in the most unlikely
circumstances and with the most unlikely people.

Abraham's flashes of faith are rightly praised by later
biblical authors. But was there ever a more fickle, wavering,
doubting man than Abraham? In this respect he is representative of all of Israel, the nation that comes forth from his
loins. Like father, like sons. If Abraham deserts the Promised
Land because of famine, so does his family two generations
hence. Abraham's sojourn in Egypt was but a few years;
Israel's was four hundred. Sarah may have been a concubine
to Pharaoh, but the people of Israel were his slaves. Yet there

was one difference: the later Pharaoh had no reason to expel this people from his land. The story of Israel in Egypt is one of increasing oppression over four centuries.

If the Abraham story highlights his addiction to order and control, the Israel story highlights the paradoxical consequences of that addiction.

⚬⚬⚬

We see a precursor after the man and the woman ate of the knowledge tree. The Lord tells the woman that as a result of her desire to rule her own life, "Your desire shall be for your husband, and he shall rule over you" (Gen. 3:16). The relationship between man and woman had been characterized by equality. She was made of the same stuff as man. She was described as bone of his bone and flesh of his flesh. She was a partner in tending the garden. But all that is academic now.

From this point on their history, and the history of gender, the history of all human relations, is characterized by oppression and struggle. History is the monotonous tale of the rise and fall of great civilizations—of growing power, control, and oppression of one group, followed by that of another. The language of liberation is often used to justify the overthrow of one regime, but it is not long before oppression characterizes the rule of the "liberators."

This is why twentieth-century novelist, essayist, and critic George Orwell said, "If you want a vision of the future, imagine a boot stamping on a human face—forever."[1]

The people of Israel go to Egypt to be saved from famine. But after the famine, they do not return to the land promised them. Things are apparently good. They have secure jobs; they know the best places to shop; they have found family physicians they like; the place feels like home. Some of their elders remind them of the promise made to Abraham and his son Isaac and Isaac's son Jacob, but after another generation, this seems like a fairy tale. That land is no more ripe for the taking than it had ever been, still filled with Canaanites and others. In comparison, Egypt is their Promised Land. This is as good as it is going to get.

When the people first arrived, they lived under the rule of a benevolent Pharaoh. But human nature being what it is, it doesn't take long before benevolence slowly evaporates in the heat of rule. By the time a few centuries have slipped by, the Israelites find themselves under a Pharaoh who fears them. They have indeed been fruitful and have multiplied in this land, and Pharaoh does not like it one bit. He worries that their numbers will become so large they will become a fifth column or perhaps decide to up and leave. In any case, Egypt's economy has become dependent on their labor, and their departure would spell disaster for Pharaoh.

By their nature, despots have limited imaginations. The book of Exodus describes Pharaoh's creative solution:

> Therefore they set taskmasters over them to afflict them with heavy burdens. They built for Pharaoh store cities, Pithom and Raamses. But the more they were oppressed, the more they multiplied and the more they spread abroad. And the Egyptians were in dread of the people of Israel. So they ruthlessly made the people of Israel work as slaves and made their lives bitter with hard service, in mortar and brick, and in all kinds of work in the field. In all their work they ruthlessly made them work as slaves. (Exod. 1:11–14)

The writer makes sure we get the point by repeating "made them work as slaves," but the point is made without the repetition. The point is actually better made in the next part of the story, when the Hebrew midwives are ordered by the authorities to murder all newborn males. Oppressors characteristically thwart the divine command and the natural inclination of living beings to be fruitful and multiply; oppressors don't like anything out of their control, and they always try to bring the chaotic thing called life to heel. But the bottom line is this: the land that Israel had looked to for liberation has become a gulag.

"Serves them right," would be an understandable and justifiable reaction of the God who longed to be their God in the land of his choosing. But this God who is hardly oblivious to the gravity of their actions—he often reacts to it as if it signals their death—nonetheless acts as if something greater is at stake. As he will do time and again, he starts scheming to liberate them.

He begins by saving a Hebrew from the death grip of Pharaoh and even arranging for him—a young man named Moses—to be raised in the very house of oppression. Early on Moses feels the call of liberation on his life, but like Abraham, rather than wait for the time and place allotted him by Providence, he takes matters into his own hands. One day he murders an Egyptian, which does nothing but put a price on his head. He flees Egypt for Midian, abandoning his revolutionary aspirations. He finds a wife and becomes a gentleman herder in the country, far from the political intrigues of Egypt.

Even when it is God's time and place, Moses manages to bungle things. Rather than respond in trust to the call—given out of a miraculous burning bush—Moses resists. Though God promises to provide everything he needs to liberate his people, Moses makes excuse after excuse.

God, being God, gets his way, of course. And the story proceeds in gruesome fashion, for if resurrection cannot happen without death, neither can liberation. Exodus describes natural disasters and plagues that afflict the land and people and one particularly dark night after which the firstborn male in every house in Egypt is found dead. And if this were not enough, it is followed by the drowning of Pharaoh's army. But the people are finally liberated.

As is typical of this God, he calls his people into freedom in the most unlikely place. The wilderness into which Israel has been led is, to be sure, a place free from the clutches of Pharaoh, but not from the fear of hunger and thirst. Naturally, the people find it unimaginable that they can trust in a

God who has led them into desolation, and so they complain about their prospects and long for the orderly life they had in Egypt. But the God who wills to provide gives them water out of rocks and bread from heaven, day in and day out—every day a miracle of provision.

When the people finally stare at the formidable enemies who occupy their land, with their fortified cities of unscalable walls, with armies trained in the art of combat, they faint from despair. More provision, more divine intervention, more promises fulfilled, and the land is eventually theirs.

As the Bible relates, there is still no happily ever after. In the land of promise, the people cannot bear to bring themselves to live in freedom with their Liberator. Instead of living in daily trust of his provision and guidance, they are constantly taking matters into their own hands. The pattern was set in the wilderness, when at one point they got tired of waiting for Moses to bring back the commands of God, and so set up their own religion, right on the spot—making a golden calf and worshiping it—to give them the sense of transcendence and security they longed for. The pattern continues in the Promised Land, and instead of giving themselves to the liberating commands of God that have, in fact, been revealed, they give themselves time and again to religions of their own making, to gods created by their own hands.

As with most attempts to control destiny, this comes to no good, and it isn't long before the yearning for order and control creates conditions in which the people find themselves not only rent asunder by internal divisions (into two nations, Judah and Israel) but again under the thumbscrews of other rulers. And once again, God seems to have not learned his lesson, as he continues to pursue the stupid and the stubborn who find themselves once again politically oppressed. But the worse things get, the higher God raises the stakes.

The setting is this: Around 745 BC, Tiglath-Pileser III ascended the Assyrian throne and ruthlessly expanded the territory of Assyria to the west and south. He was bent on building a great empire. In his path stood the northern kingdom, Israel, but it wasn't much of a threat. It had been weakened by assassinations and ineffective leadership, so the northern kingdom was not prepared to deal with the Assyrian threat. In 734, Tiglath-Pileser's armies marched along the coast, around Israel and Judah, to cut off any assistance Egypt might offer from the south, and then turned north to attack Israel. Within a year, Assyria held the coastal areas, the northern territories of Israel (which included Naphtali, on the Sea of Galilee, and Zebulun). Assyria was now ready to pounce on Samaria, the northern capital. About this time, Ahaz became the ruler of Judah, the southern kingdom.

In this context comes a prophet named Isaiah, who describes a vision God has given him. He announces the liberation of Zebulun and Naphtali in a "latter time," when the Lord will make an escape by way of the sea (which Assyria had effectively blocked) (Isa. 9:1). Then come a series of phrases that are rightly applied to the coming Messiah but which had their original meaning in the context of Assyria's political oppression:

> The people who walked in darkness
>   have seen a great light;
> those who dwelt in a land of deep darkness,
>   on them has light shined. . . .
>
> For the yoke of his burden,
>   and the staff for his shoulder,
>   the rod of his oppressor,
> you have broken as on the day of Midian.
>   (Isa. 9:2, 4)

The occupation of Assyria is not benevolent by any means; it is described as a burdensome yoke and an oppressive rod.

And in the following line, the experience of Assyria's assault on Israel is pictured as the "boot of the tramping warrior in battle tumult" and as garments "rolled in blood" (Isa. 9:5). To be conquered by this particularly ruthless enemy must have been a horrific event.

These allusions to oppression become the background of the passage's larger point: the liberation of Israel. The burdensome yoke and oppressive rod will be broken "as on the day of Midian" (Isa. 9:4). The reference is to another moment when Israel was liberated from another oppressor, that time through the leadership of Gideon (see Judg. 6 and 7).

In addition, the tramping boot and bloody garment "will be burned as fuel for the fire." The vision looks forward to a coming liberator: "For to us a child is born, to us a son is given; and the government shall be upon his shoulder." His reign will be so just that he will be characterized as "Wonderful," "Mighty," "Everlasting." This "Prince of Peace"—who is so effective that he will be compared to God himself—will establish and uphold this new, liberated political order "with justice and with righteousness from this time forth and forevermore" (Isa. 9:5–7).

As the Bible eventually reveals, more than political liberation is on the line. At some point in the future, something extraordinary will take place, something that will reveal liberation in depth and breadth and show God to be—despite all the evidence to the contrary—the God who has been not only *for* but *with* this people all along.

7

A VARIETY OF RELIGIOUS OPPRESSION

Political oppression, it turns out, was only the proverbial tip of the iceberg. This people whom God had created for freedom and love time and again created circumstances in which life became mostly oppression and law. One of the more ironic developments is the constant recurrence of religious oppression.

On the one hand, the Bible recognizes that life in God has no meaning if it is not embedded in religious activity: Scripture study, worship, ritual, and so forth. In the Sermon on the Mount, Jesus—the "Wonderful Counselor, Mighty God, Everlasting Father, Prince of Peace" whom Isaiah pointed to (9:6)—assumed that the devout life will include prayer, fasting, and almsgiving.[1] The Bible shows that Jesus was a man of prayer (see for example Mark 1:35) and that he was a regular church attender: "And as was his custom, he went to the synagogue on the Sabbath day," notes Luke early in Jesus's ministry (4:16).

At the same time, the Bible can talk about religion as if it were the enemy. We're not just talking about false religion or idol worship, against which prophets like Isaiah could wax eloquent and sarcastic.[2] The prophets could also indict perfectly acceptable religious practices. Take for example Isaiah's classic charge, when he quotes God as saying:

> When you come to appear before me,
>   who has required of you
>   this trampling of my courts?
> Bring no more vain offerings;
>   incense is an abomination to me.
> New moon and Sabbath and the calling of
>   convocations—
>   I cannot endure iniquity and solemn assembly.
> Your new moons and your appointed feasts
>   my soul hates;
> they have become a burden to me;
>   I am weary of bearing them. (Isa. 1:12–14)

This must have been shocking rhetoric in Isaiah's day, because offerings and feasts and religious gatherings are so much of what biblical books like Leviticus are all about. The people were doing in spades the exact thing they were commanded to do.

Religion as such is not the problem, only religion that becomes an excuse for or even a means of social and economic oppression. God despises religion when people use it to avoid some rather elementary matters of justice. Take one passage from the prophet Micah:

> Hear this, you heads of the house of Jacob
>   and rulers of the house of Israel,
> who detest justice
>   and make crooked all that is straight,
> who build Zion with blood
>   and Jerusalem with iniquity.

> Its heads give judgment for a bribe;
>> its priests teach for a price;
>> its prophets practice divination for money.
>>> (Mic. 3:9–11)

This type of oppression goes hand in hand with political oppression, but in this case, religion does not question but supports the oppressive order.

People look to political leaders to bring order and peace, but time and again in history, those leaders overdo it. Sometimes the people let them, so fearful are they of aliens across the border or troublemakers in their midst. When a people is fearful, they give more and more power to government and slowly but surely find themselves less and less free. Political leaders, each tempted by power as much as you or I might be, are more than happy to take the reins, which eventually they turn into whips.

In the same way, people look to religious leaders to bring order and peace to their spiritual lives. And they are willing to pay good money to know what God thinks of this and that. It starts out justly enough; the laborer is worthy of his hire even if the laborer is working in the fields of the Lord. But it doesn't take long before the money is the main thing and religion is merely a means to that end. Pretty soon pastors are opening up wedding chapels (a brisk little business) and going on speaking tours (a lucrative big business), teaching for a price, and offering spiritual counsel for money. And people are so desperate for moral and spiritual order, they'll pay the extortion.

The solution to such religion is not to abandon it but to fulfill it; that is, to use religion to inspire not works of mammon but of mercy:

> Is not this the fast that I choose:
>> to loose the bonds of wickedness,
>> to undo the straps of the yoke,
> to let the oppressed go free,
>> and to break every yoke? (Isa. 58:6)

71

In short, God's mission when it comes to religious oppression is the same as his mission when it comes to political oppression: liberation.

❦

In the biblical story, we see that religion gets twisted by people in other ways, for instance into moral oppression. This is a recurring theme of Jesus's interaction with the religious leaders of his day. One classic encounter happens when one group of religious leaders, the Pharisees, defenders of the moral order, criticize Jesus and his disciples for plucking grain on the Sabbath. In that day, this was a technical violation of Sabbath rules. But Jesus will have none of it. He is not one to bend the knee to moral law just because it is moral law. Jesus knows that to enslave oneself to the letter is a refusal to live by the Spirit.

Jesus's pithy response gets to the heart of the matter: "The Sabbath was made for man, not man for the Sabbath" (Mark 2:27). The point of this religious law, as with all religious law, is not found in itself. No, the law is designed to bring freedom and life.

There is no more succinct expression of Jesus's exasperation with moral oppression than his famous sermon against the Pharisees, which begins,

> The scribes and the Pharisees sit on Moses' seat, so practice and observe whatever they tell you—but not what they do. For they preach, but do not practice. They tie up heavy burdens, hard to bear, and lay them on people's shoulders, but they themselves are not willing to move them with their finger. (Matt. 23:2–4)

The apostle Paul is one with his master in this. His letter to the church in Galatia is very much in the spirit of Jesus's sermon against the Pharisees. In this case, it is new Christians who make the law an end in itself, who use law to burden instead of to free people. Some Christians were arguing that accepting circumcision was part and parcel of being a Christian. They assumed that since God's covenant with Abraham included circumcision, God's covenant in Christ would require the same.

Paul responds with a decided "No!" arguing in so many words that what had once been a sign of God's gracious relationship with his people had become—as we have seen time and again—a mere external ritual. Instead of it being a free act of gratitude for God's goodness, it had become a religious yardstick for measuring one's righteousness. This is not freedom but moral oppression. Paul will have none of it:

> For freedom Christ has set us free; stand firm therefore, and do not submit again to a yoke of slavery. . . . For in Christ Jesus neither circumcision nor uncircumcision counts for anything, but only faith working through love. (Gal. 5:1, 6)

With the coming of Jesus Christ, every law and commandment is turned on its head. They are not ends in themselves but means to an end—a life of freedom and love.

We've jumped ahead a bit. As suggested above, the story of the Bible hinges on one particular story within it, the story of Jesus Christ. It is the story that ties together all the stories—from Adam and Eve to Abraham and Sarah to Moses and Isaiah to Paul and the Galatians, clear through to the end of time. And it is nothing but a story of liberation.

We see this in the many stories in which Jesus delivers people from sickness and demonic oppression. Time and again, people who are "oppressed by demons" come to him to be freed from illness, which Jesus understood as a type of spiritual oppression. Thus when Jesus commissions his disciples to share in his work, he sums up that work in this way: "Heal the sick, raise the dead, cleanse lepers, cast out demons" (Matt. 10:8).

Spiritual oppression takes another, even more debilitating form. Jesus frames his ministry in this light in the middle of the Gospel of John:

> If you abide in my word, you are truly my disciples, and you will know the truth, and the truth will set you free. . . . Truly, truly, I say to you, everyone who commits sin is a slave to sin. The slave does not remain in the house forever; the son remains forever. So if the Son sets you free, you will be free indeed. (8:31–32, 34–36)

Paul put it this way in his letter to the Romans:

> We know that our old self was crucified with him in order that the body of sin might be brought to nothing, so that we would no longer be enslaved to sin. For one who has died has been set free from sin. Now if we have died with Christ, we believe that we will also live with him. (6:6–8)

The sin that Jesus and Paul note took its first form in the eating of the forbidden fruit, followed by the murder of a brother. Then we see it manifested in Abraham's repeated refusal to trust in God's promise and provision, and in Moses's impatience to get on with his call. Sin is the refusal to live in loving trust in God's daily word, which is freedom itself. It is refusal to be fruitful and multiply, to tend to garden work, to live calmly and trustingly when God's order seems to be on the verge of chaos. It is impatience about living from daily provision of manna, and it is building altars to golden calves when God seems not to speak quickly enough. Sin takes the commandment of God and turns it into an iron rule rather than a living word from a loving Creator, something we control rather than something that controls us. Sin is the yearning to live safe, controlled, predictable lives instead of lives born in and driven by the wild and unpredictable Spirit of God. Sin is fundamentally a desire for order where God does not want order and to control that which God does not want us to control.

And not surprisingly, what comes of this panting after order and control is that our lives are ordered and controlled by that which cannot give life: spiritual oppression. Sin enslaves the person who participates in it. It's spiritual heroin. It is something we do because we think it will increase our options, but it soon narrows them to the point of death. And the tragedy is that when we realize the trajectory that our sin has put us on and try to break away from its grip, we discover that its grip becomes stronger than ever. We are powerless over our addiction, an addiction from which only death itself could set us free.

Dealing with this oppression—the oppression in which all oppression finds its root—was the mission of God in Jesus Christ. Liberation from the oppression of sin required a death, but in a gift as mysterious as it is wonderful, it was the death of Jesus—the Wonderful Counselor, Mighty God, Everlasting Father, Prince of Peace—that has made the difference.

Gift is the key word here, according to Paul in Romans:

> Therefore, just as sin came into the world through one man, and death through sin, and so death spread to all men because all sinned. . . . But the *free gift* is not like the trespass. For if many died through one man's trespass, much more have the grace of God and the *free gift* by the grace of that one man Jesus Christ abounded for many. . . . For if, because of one man's trespass, death reigned through that one man, much more will those who receive the abundance of grace and the *free gift* of righteousness reign in life through the one man Jesus Christ. (Rom. 5:12, 15, 17, emphasis added)

What Christ has done is not obligation. It is not duty. It is not a quid pro quo, something for something. It is gift, and as gift it is an offering made in freedom. Only a free gift can bring true freedom.

To signal that he was free to give this gift of his death, and free over the gift itself, free from the curse of Adam ("for you are dust, and to dust you shall return," Gen. 3:19) that has oppressed humankind since, Christ overcame death and rose from the grave. "For as by a man came death," writes Paul, "by a man has come also the resurrection of the dead. For as in Adam all die, so also in Christ shall all be made alive" (1 Cor. 15:21–22).

It is no wonder that when Paul tries to sum up all of who Christ is and all that he has done for us, his words cascade over one another: "For freedom Christ has set us free" (Gal. 5:1)!

Paul is not the only one who sums up Jesus's work in this way. At the very beginning of his ministry, Jesus went to the synagogue to explain the work he was about to embark on. He quoted a passage from the prophet Isaiah and in doing so, pointed to himself:

> The Spirit of the Lord is upon me,
>   because he has anointed me
>   to proclaim good news to the poor.
> He has sent me to proclaim liberty to the captives
>   and recovering of sight to the blind,
>   to set at liberty those who are oppressed. (Luke
>   4:18)

Jesus announced that overcoming oppression in whatever form it comes—political, economic, moral, or spiritual—was the object of his life. He is the liberating Son of a liberating Father, who then sent a liberating Spirit to complete the work.

Even in his ministry, Jesus already was showing what that liberating work looks like.

8

JESUS THE LIBERATOR

God made an extraordinary statement when he came in Jesus—"Mighty God" in the flesh. It was a quiet and humble entrance; he was born as a babe in a manger, in the context of family. But it was framed by the same holy chaos that the Spirit introduced into the world in the beginning. As such, it reveals how God in Jesus, and later in the Holy Spirit, accomplishes his liberating work with a people.

Jesus's human life began, says the Bible, with a virginal conception—decidedly not in accord with the normal order of things. Then a host of angels announced the birth to startled shepherds with what would turn out to be ironic words: "Peace on earth!" (Luke 2:14 CEV). For the first memorable political act after the birth of Immanuel—"God with us"— was the mass murder of infants, followed by the exile of the holy family (see Matt. 2:13–18). Thus the first sign of God's coming led to disruption and confusion.

Even in his childhood, Jesus signaled his indifference to the status quo. He was only twelve when he disobeyed his parents, staying in the temple in Jerusalem after they had started home. In doing so, he flaunted the fifth commandment—"Honor your father and your mother" (Exod. 20:12)—apparently believing that the fifth commandment was not made for man, but man for the fifth commandment. His parents were naturally hurt: "Son, why have you treated us so?" (Luke 2:48). But Jesus just rebuked them for not recognizing his mission. Jesus was not always a good boy.

Things got really interesting when Jesus began his ministry some eighteen years later. His opening sermon announced his mission of liberation. He was in Nazareth, his hometown. He had an opportunity to win the favor of family and friends, so they could give him their blessing. Instead, he decided to shame them for their parochialism. He said that God is just as interested in sharing his mercy with Gentiles as he is in sharing it with his chosen people. You know Jesus touched a raw nerve because his friends and relatives—the people who had a natural affection for him—dragged him to the edge of town to throw him off a cliff (see Luke 4:16–30).

The pattern has been set. So we shouldn't be surprised subsequently to see Jesus time and again challenge the religious order of his day—sometimes openly flaunting custom and law. He encourages his disciples to break the Sabbath. He associates with the religiously disreputable. He welcomes women, second-class citizens in his day, to participate in his mission. He questions customs on fasting, almsgiving, and prayer (see Matt. 6; Mark 2:15, 23–28; Luke 8:1–3).

One particular incident reveals Jesus's destabilizing method (see Luke 6:6–11). One Sabbath, Jesus is teaching in the synagogue. Luke notes that in addition to the congregation, "scribes and Pharisees" are also present, as is a man whose right hand is withered. The religious leaders have come to catch Jesus breaking religious law—in particular, healing on the Sabbath.

Jesus could easily avoid a confrontation. The man with the withered hand does not ask for healing. Jesus is not obliged to heal and thus flaunt religious custom. Jesus could simply do nothing.

Further, even if he feels compelled to heal the man, there is no reason Jesus could not wait just a few hours, until the sun set. Then the Sabbath will be over, and healing will be permitted. The man has lived with this impediment for years, if not decades. He certainly could wait a few more hours to be healed. Jesus could pursue a win-win solution: heal the man, avoid working on the Sabbath, and stay on the good side of the religious leaders.

But Jesus cares little about social harmony if it thwarts the dynamic work of God. So he calls the man forward in the middle of the service, in the middle of the Sabbath, and heals him. Jesus deliberately provokes. Jesus initiates controversy. Jesus destabilizes the situation.

It is this sort of behavior that eventually gets him killed. But not before he manages to upset every expectation about God and his Messiah and the religious life.

He teaches that God is enamored not so much with the pious but with the poor, the sad, the meek, the hungry. Contrary to the common assumption that the rich have been divinely blessed, Jesus says wealth is a curse. He says that rather than retaliating, one should forgive. Rather than hating enemies, one should love them. Rather than keeping what is rightfully yours, you should give it away.[1]

A man who goes about challenging the political, religious, and moral order could be mistaken for a revolutionary. And this is precisely what people think. Jesus, though, is quick to disabuse them of this. When Peter apparently assumes that Jesus's mission will only be accomplished by a military victory over Rome, Jesus calls him the incarnation of Satan. He then reminds Peter and the other disciples of the great paradox: that only in giving up one's life can one preserve and foster life (see Mark 8:31–38).

When one of the disciples tries to prevent his arrest, slashing at the soldiers who have come for him, Jesus tells him to sheath his sword.

When Jesus has a chance to defend himself before authorities who hold the power of capital punishment, he remains silent.

When unjustly tried and cruelly nailed to a cross—just when righteous anger would have been expected and justified—he openly forgives his accusers.

These are not the actions and words of a man who takes his bearings from what is expected, from what constitutes "the normal order of things." He is decidedly uninterested in preserving order, in maintaining the status quo. He says that he didn't come to abolish the law but to fulfill it. But it is impossible to ignore the fact that in fulfilling it, he transcended it, and by transcending it, he introduced chaos—"a condition or place of great disorder or confusion."

Disorder and confusion abound when we come to the end of his story. An innocent man is arrested on trumped-up charges and condemned to death. God's righteous one suffers and is crucified. A dead man rises again.

This "happy ending" only makes things more confusing. In one account, the men guarding the tomb "trembled and became like dead men" (Matt. 28:4). In another, the disciples are "startled and frightened" (Luke 24:37). In another still, two men have no idea they are conversing with Jesus (Luke 24:13–35). The characteristic response to the resurrection is that of the women, who Mark says "fled from the tomb, for trembling and astonishment had seized them, and they said nothing to anyone, for they were afraid" (Mark 16:8).

In the centuries since, Christians have tried to tame the resurrection, shoring it up with logical and historical proofs, talking about it as if it makes perfect sense. But a resurrection that has become a comforting tale is not the resurrection of Jesus Christ. The resurrection of Jesus announces a new world order, doing so first by upsetting and demolishing the old world order. It is not the mere resuscitation of a body, but a signal that everything that is dead—predictable, rigid, lifeless, and orderly—is going to be made unpredictable, flexible, lively, and new.

That's the type of thing holy chaos does. It shatters the order that has become oppressive. It throws out of kilter that which had been tightly controlled. It forces everyone to make a choice: hold on tighter to a life made in our image, or let go and see the new, liberating thing God is doing.

This disruptive, resurrection life only spread after Jesus left and gave us the Holy Spirit—the one we first saw brooding and creating mischief on the formless and void planet.

9

CHAOS AND THE SPIRIT

As we've seen in the creation, the Spirit revealed something of God's mischievous character. I did not say so explicitly, but it was the Spirit who was also behind the work of those crazy prophets like Isaiah and Micah, who burned eloquent against the political and religious oppression of their day and who announced the coming liberation in the one called "Mighty God." It was the Spirit who empowered the holy chaotic work of Jesus, and it was the Spirit who Jesus specifically noted would carry on the work of liberation after he departed.

The ongoing liberating work of the Spirit is first revealed in the book typically titled "The Acts of the Apostles." But this is a misnomer. While it does show the apostles acting, more times than not it shows them responding to the unsettling work of the Spirit.

For example, despite the fact that they are told to be witnesses "in Jerusalem and in all Judea and Samaria and to the end of the earth" (Acts 1:8), they take no initiative leaving

Jerusalem. It takes a providential persecution before Jesus's followers are dispersed, and even then the apostles hold back: "And there arose on that day a great persecution against the church in Jerusalem, and they were all scattered throughout the regions of Judea and Samaria, *except the apostles*" (Acts 8:1, emphasis added).

Other examples will soon be discussed. The book, therefore, should not be called "The Acts of the Apostles" as much as "The Hesitation of the Apostles." Or better, because the actor in this book is the Holy Spirit, "The Acts of the Holy Spirit."

Luke, the author of Acts, begins by noting that this is the second part of a larger work, the first part being about "all that Jesus *began* to do and teach" (1:1, emphasis added). The implication is that the book of Acts is the *continuation* of what Jesus did and taught.

Yet within a few verses, Luke says Jesus ascended to heaven. How can the book now be about the continuing works and teaching *of Jesus*? The point, of course, is that the ministry of Jesus continues in the Holy Spirit.

Earlier in the Bible, Jesus is equated with "Mighty God," the presence of God with his people. Luke continues this association when in Acts he conflates Jesus's role and power with that of God. Jesus is said to sit at God's right hand (see 2:33). Throughout the book, Jesus is called by names usually given to God alone, like "the Holy and Righteous One" (3:14) and "the Author of life" (3:15).

So what does this mean? In the end, the church concluded that there is no essential difference between the Father and the Son, nor the Son and the Spirit. In essence each is God. Thus the acts of the Holy Spirit are at the same time the acts of Jesus and the acts of the Father.

Three key moments early in the life of the church signal that the God of liberation is at work in the Holy Spirit. The first and most dramatic comes on the day of Pentecost.

The event is set in a religious custom. Jews from across the world had gathered in Jerusalem. Pentecost—also called the Feast of Weeks—was one of the major feasts of the Jewish year. It was one of three obligatory observances for Jews, falling between the feasts of Passover and Tabernacles. Originally it was called "the Feast of Harvest, of the firstfruits of your labor, of what you sow in the field" (Exod. 23:16) and then later it was known as the feast of "the firstfruits of wheat harvest" (Exod. 34:22).

But by the time of our story, in Acts 2, it had lost its association with agriculture and had become an occasion to remember the giving of the Torah to Israel. Thus in both form (an annual religious ritual) and in content (the celebration of the Law), it is an event about liturgical and moral order. It is no coincidence that at *this* festival, the Holy Spirit came with power and disorder.

First comes "from heaven a sound like a mighty rushing wind, and it filled the entire house where they were sitting" (v. 2). Then appear "divided tongues as of fire" that "rested on" each of them (v. 3). Luke is clearly grasping for the right words, for the scene is impossible to visualize.

Then comes the audible miracle. People from across that portion of the world (sixteen people groups are mentioned) exclaim, "We hear them telling in our own tongues the mighty works of God" (v. 11). This miracle brings not peace and order but only amazement and perplexity. Witnesses took it for a drunken party (vv. 12–13).

As noted earlier, this does not reverse what happened to the people of Shinar. On the day of Pentecost, people do not lose the gift of multiple languages. There seem to be as many languages spoken as there are people groups present: "We hear them telling in our own tongues the mighty works of God" (v. 11). The holy diversity remains.

What's new is this: the gift of language is now not merely about diversity of culture but the means by which God makes his works known. One of those works is the very presence of diverse languages and cultures, in fulfillment of God's command to be fruitful and multiply. But of course, Luke strongly implies (based on Peter's following sermon) that the main "mighty work of God" is the announcement of God's disruptive and redemptive work in Jesus Christ.

Peter explains, quoting the prophet Joel, that the confusion people are seeing is the wave of the future:

> And in the last days it shall be, God declares,
>   that I will pour out my Spirit on all flesh,
>   and your sons and your daughters shall prophesy,
>   and your young men shall see visions,
>   and your old men shall dream dreams;
> even on my male servants and female servants
>   in those days I will pour out my Spirit, and they
>   shall prophesy. (2:17–18)

In this remarkable statement, Peter announces that the religious and social order is being completely upended. The Spirit will now come upon "all flesh," not just prophets and priests. Specifically "young men" and "male servants" and "daughters" and even the lowest in the social hierarchy, "female servants," will experience this. Everyone, from the top to the bottom of the social hierarchy, has access to the wondrous Spirit of God.

The religion of the future, implies Peter, will be a religion of the Spirit and a religion of the heart. And that future is now. This religion is not about external law and ritual; it is not about a priestly class and a lay class; it is not about institutions and programs. It is about "the law written on the heart" (see Rom. 2:15) and the Spirit filling *every* believer.

This does not do away with religion. The book of Acts, after all, is about the creation of the institution called the church. But religion is now relativized. There is no Christian faith without the institutional church, but the institution is not the Christian faith. The institution is merely the playground in which to enjoy the freedom of God; it is the canvas upon which God paints with broad strokes the miracle of divine love.

Peter says what is happening is the result of another astonishing event: What could be more confusing to a devout Jew than the idea of the Messiah shamefully dying on a cross? And what could be more unnerving to those Jews who did not believe in resurrection, and to Greeks who thought resurrection a myth, than to be told that Jesus was raised from the dead?

Jesus brings confusion layered upon disorder leading to a complete reversal in so many matters. It is the height of theological absurdity for Peter to say, "Let all the house of Israel therefore know for certain that God has made him both Lord and Christ, this Jesus whom you crucified" (2:36). It is no wonder that when the Spirit descends upon people, the same sort of holy chaos—strange tongues!—results.

And yet, those willing to have their worlds turned upside down, those willing to follow where the wild Spirit leads—those who repent and believe, to use Peter's language—will be forgiven their sins (freed from guilt) and liberated from the need for order and control; that is, freed to live a life in obedience to God's liberating command.

The Spirit is a gift of ongoing chaos in the church. This gift points not only backward—to the life, death, and resurrection of Jesus—but forward to the confused, chaotic freedom and love that characterizes the life in the church.

The connection between chaos and liberation is seen nearly every time the apostles preach. For example, after Peter and John heal a paralytic, people are filled with "wonder and amazement"—what we might call happy confusion (3:10). The miraculous by its very nature upsets the natural order. But Peter only makes things "worse" when he opens his mouth to explain from whence came the power to heal:

The God of Abraham, the God of Isaac, and the God of Jacob, the God of our fathers, glorified his servant Jesus, whom you delivered over and denied in the presence of Pilate, when he had decided to release him. But you denied the Holy and Righteous One, and asked for a murderer to be granted to you, and you killed the Author of life, whom God raised from the dead. (3:13–15)

Peter says the Messiah—"the Holy and Righteous One" and "the Author of life"—was killed. The one whose holiness and righteousness should have guaranteed his safety, the one who is master of life and death—this one was murdered. And the people who think of themselves as devout were the very ones who did the killing. If this sort of logic does not theologically confuse these listeners, it's hard to imagine what would.

And as if that were not enough, Peter kicks the already upset apple cart, announcing that the one who was killed— which should have been a sign of judgment for his sin—was made alive and vindicated by the Holy Judge.

After Peter later makes a similar speech before the authorities, Luke writes, "Now when they saw the boldness of Peter and John, and perceived that they were uneducated, common men, they were astonished" (4:13).

It's not just preaching but prayer that literally shakes people up. After one gathering, Luke notes, "And when they had prayed, the place in which they were gathered together was shaken, and they were all filled with the Holy Spirit" (4:31).

As we rummage through the book of Acts, the Holy Spirit upends not just theology and religion. The Spirit's work is always a personal work.

Stephen is introduced as a deacon, that is, as one called to the quiet, practical, and sensible ministry of serving widows. But the Holy Spirit rewrites Stephen's job description, which seems to have consisted of distributing food on a daily basis.

This delivery man is described as "full of grace and power" and as one who "was doing great wonders and signs among the people" (6:8).

To that Stephen adds discombobulating speech, which only gets him arrested. In the course of a speech defending himself, he makes the same absurd claims about Jesus as did Peter. This only infuriates his accusers, who stone him to death.

Later Philip proclaims Christ in Samaria, performing signs and wonders: "For unclean spirits, crying with a loud voice, came out of many who had them, and many who were paralyzed or lame were healed" (8:7). Then suddenly he is told by "an angel of the Lord" to leave this ministry (which is bearing joyful fruit) and to make his way into the desert (8:26). There he meets an Ethiopian official, engages him in conversation, and finally baptizes him. After which, Luke says, "the Spirit of the Lord carried Philip away. . . . Philip found himself at Azotus" (8:39–40). Whether Luke intends some sort of supernatural transport or merely a metaphorical description of the Spirit's guidance, the point is clear: Philip's life is shaken up time and again by the Spirit's leading.

Then there is the experience of Peter in Acts 10. For him holy chaos comes in the form of a vision. He has been praying and has become hungry when he falls "into a trance" (v. 10). He sees a great sheet descending from heaven upon which are "all kinds of animals and reptiles and birds of the air" (v. 12).

Then a voice says, "Rise, Peter; kill and eat" (v. 13).

This is something of a shock to the devout Jew Peter. Like his fellow religionists, he had made it a point not to eat things forbidden by Mosaic law. Consequently he replies, "By no means, Lord; for I have never eaten anything that is common or unclean" (v. 14).

To which the voice responds, "What God has made clean, do not call common" (v. 15).

This happens three times, and afterward, Luke says, "Peter was inwardly perplexed as to what the vision that he had seen might mean" (v. 17).

At that point, Peter receives a visit from servants of a centurion named Cornelius, a Gentile, who have come to invite Peter to his home. This invitation would normally have resulted in a polite refusal, because as Peter put it later, it is "unlawful . . . for a Jew to associate with or to visit anyone of another nation" (v. 28). But the Holy Spirit is shaking things up, and Peter recognizes that something holy is in the confusion. So he goes.

The end result is not only the conversion of Cornelius to Christ, but Peter's conversion to Christ's mission: "Truly I understand that God shows no partiality" (v. 34). This may be a common idea to modern sensibilities, but for a devout Jew, faithful to the letter of the Mosaic law, this is about as radical as it gets.

By this time, the quintessential disturbance of the Spirit had already occurred on the road to Damascus. On a mission to end the disruption caused by the Christians was one Saul. He was an admired figure of his day, a member of the strict Pharisees, zealous for the tradition, meticulous in keeping the law.

Saul had been deeply troubled by the rise of a new sect called the Way. Saul recognized that their message, if spread, could shake his religion to its foundations. So he gave himself to rooting out these disturbers of the peace, hunting them down and, if necessary, killing them.

He is on his way to Damascus to do just that ("breathing threats and murder" as Luke puts it in 9:1) when the foundation of his own life cracks open. He is thrown to the ground by a bright light and a loud voice. The man who thought he saw all things clearly is blinded. Three days later his sight is restored, but his view of the world has completely changed.

He is no longer an enemy but an apostle of Jesus Christ. He is no longer merely a Jew but a world citizen.

The chaos that interrupted and transformed the lives of Peter and Paul eventually makes its way into a church council—where there is "no small dissension and debate" (15:2) about what place Gentiles have in the life of the church of Jesus Christ. The Council of Jerusalem is the first church-wide gathering to settle a matter that had been brought to their attention by the unsettling work of the Spirit.

This becomes the pattern for church life since.

10

LIBERATION STARTS WITH CHAOS

Since the book of Acts, the Spirit has been disturbing the church. To pick out just four events of holy chaos: the early councils that wrestled with the nature of Jesus; the Reformation that highlighted the miracle of grace and faith; the nineteenth century—the missions century—that reordered church priorities with the Great Commission; and the twentieth-century Pentecostal movement, which has dramatically reshaped the map of world Christianity. We see lots of chaos in church history. And lots of grace.

Chaos is the work of the Spirit, who disturbs the status quo, whether that status quo is political, social, religious, or spiritual. Chaos reveals the excessive order and forces us to make a decision—either to grasp ever harder to control or to let our lives be led by the Spirit.

Such is the point of some types of political action, especially when used in the service of liberation. Take for example the civil disobedience of Martin Luther King Jr. In his famous

"Letter from a Birmingham Jail," King explains to fellow clergymen why he has organized marches and sit-ins and other protests that "disturbed the peace":

> You may well ask: "Why direct action? Why sit-ins, marches and so forth? Isn't negotiation a better path?" You are quite right in calling for negotiation. Indeed, this is the very purpose of direct action. Nonviolent direct action seeks to create such a crisis and foster such a tension that a community which has constantly refused to negotiate is forced to confront the issue. It seeks so to dramatize the issue that it can no longer be ignored.

He explains that while he opposes *violent* tension, he believes there is "a type of constructive, nonviolent tension which is necessary for growth":

> Just as Socrates felt that it was necessary to create a tension in the mind so that individuals could rise from the bondage of myths and half-truths to the unfettered realm of creative analysis and objective appraisal, so must we see the need for nonviolent gadflies to create the kind of tension in society that will help men rise from the dark depths of prejudice and racism to the majestic heights of understanding and brotherhood.

He concludes this portion of the letter by explaining that the purpose of the protests is "to create a situation so crisis-packed that it will inevitably open the door to negotiation."[1]

The peace that he disturbed was no peace, but instead a quiet but ruthless oppression of blacks. And the Birmingham clergy, as much as the rest of the city's established order, were guilty of maintaining an unhealthy, sinful control over that order. A crisis needed to be created that not only exposed the oppression but also cast a beam of light that pointed to liberation, in this case, "the majestic heights of understanding and brotherhood."

Such is the way of the liberating work of the Spirit. It begins in chaos, creating a tension that so disturbs the status quo that it leads to a crisis, which in turn exposes the oppression and opens the possibility of liberation.

Let's look at it from a personal perspective. God calls us to order our days according to his will and for his glory. But how easily do such plans become merely our plans—inflexible, stubborn things that not even God can interrupt! Dietrich Bonhoeffer, in his classic *Life Together*, writes about this common human experience:

> We must be ready to allow ourselves to be interrupted by God. God will be constantly crossing our paths and canceling our plans by sending us people with claims and petitions. We may pass them by, preoccupied with our more important tasks, as the priest passed by the man who had fallen among thieves, perhaps reading the Bible. When we do that we pass by the visible sign of the Cross raised athwart our path to show us that not our way but God's way must be done.

He says that when we refuse to let nothing disturb our plans, we are disdaining God's "crooked yet straight path."[2]

It is the work of the Spirit—especially when excessive control reigns—to make the straight paths crooked, to upset the established order, to introduce chaos, even interrupting our schedules, and thus opening us to the possibility of liberation.

John Brown, the nineteenth-century abolitionist, fought for the same things as did Martin Luther King Jr. The difference, of course, is that Brown was a terrorist. He was not averse to using violence against the innocent to introduce tension into an oppressive racist order. We rightly reject his terrorism, but not his motives.

In 1859, Brown attempted to start a slave insurrection, which failed miserably. He was apprehended, tried, and sentenced to death. During the trial, he explained his actions:

This court acknowledges, as I suppose, the validity of the law of God. I see a book kissed here which I suppose to be the Bible, or at least the New Testament. That teaches me that all things whatsoever I would that men should do to me, I should do even so to them. It teaches me, further, to "remember them that are in bonds, as bound with them."

He said that if he had to give up his life "for the furtherance of the ends of justice," seeking liberation for the millions of slaves "whose rights are disregarded by wicked, cruel, and unjust enactments, I submit; so let it be done!"[3]

That phrase from the King James Version—to "remember them that are in bonds, as bound with them" (Heb. 13:3)—captures the essence of the Christian calling. It is grounded in a profound connectedness with other human beings suffering any sort of oppression—from the political to the physical to the spiritual. Oppression in its various and sundry forms is so entrenched and widespread, the work of liberation can demand nothing less than our whole heart, soul, mind, and strength. There is no greater love than that we should give our lives for brothers and sisters who are enslaved to the yoke of tyranny, especially spiritual tyranny.

The demand of this call is precisely why, when we are presented with it, we flinch. The classic example is that of Moses.

After Moses approaches the burning bush, he discovers not only that he is in the presence of the Lord God, but that the Lord has a mission for him:

> Behold, the cry of the people of Israel has come to me, and I have also seen the oppression with which the Egyptians oppress them. Come, I will send you to Pharaoh that you may bring my people, the children of Israel, out of Egypt. (Exod. 3:9–10).

Moses wonders how he, a mere country shepherd, can challenge the entrenched power of the world's greatest empire—and he reacts accordingly: "Who am I that I should go

to Pharaoh and bring the children of Israel out of Egypt?"
(Exod. 3:11).

Whether the call is to the world's most powerful empire or
to speak a word of grace into the life of someone oppressed by
guilt, it can be an intimidating moment. Who are we to effect
liberation? Really, what can mere words do—puffs of sound,
floating through air until they collapse in helpless silence—to
assure the guilt-stricken that they really are forgiven? How
can serving a meal to the homeless alter in any significant
and lasting way the fact and psychology of homelessness?
What can one person do in the face of global inequities and
tyranny? An honest person, a humble person, can do nothing
but what Moses did and ask, "Who am I?"

It is interesting to note that the Lord does not argue
this point. He does not try to pump up Moses's flagging
self-esteem with positive bromides: "Moses, don't be silly.
You can do it! You have innate gifts and abilities, which I
have given you. Just concentrate on your strengths!" and
so on and so forth. Instead of encouraging Moses with
empty talk of possibility thinking, he gives him something
he can really hold on to, something that will make all the
difference.

God says, "But I will be with you" (Exod. 3:12).

The work of liberation is God's work first and last. He
initiates it. He carries it out. He finishes it. He uses the likes
of Moses, and the likes of us, to do this work. But it is grace
that makes it possible for us to participate in his great work,
and it is God's initiative and power that make it possible for
us to imagine we might even succeed.

The human mind, being what it is, still balks. "How do I
know this is true? How can I know that not only the call to
liberating work but also the promised liberation will come
to pass?"

The Lord anticipates this in Moses's response and, immediately after promising his abiding presence, says, "And
this shall be the sign for you, that I have sent you: when you

95

have brought the people out of Egypt, you shall serve God on this mountain" (Exod. 3:12).

Some sign! The sign is that when all is said and done, you'll be standing in this very place, far from the land of Egypt, and you and the people of Israel will be free.

That is not much of a sign; at least it's not the type of sign we long for—something that assures us *ahead of time* that what we are about to embark on is the right path, that what we set out to do at God's bidding will come to pass. Instead, the sign is a sign of faith, a sign of trust. We are called into the risky and scary work of liberation, not having any concrete assurances ahead of time that it will all pan out. No, to give such proof would undermine the very thing God is trying to do here: get us to put our full trust in the one who will be with us always. If he were to give us a proof—a miracle, a signed contract, an unshakable confidence—then we'd start trusting in the proof and not the God who gave the proof. Instead, God skips the proof and basically says, "Trust me."

This encounter between Moses and God, of course, is an example of holy chaos. Remember how Moses, like John Brown, used violence to save a couple of Israelites from the tyrannical hand of Egypt—he murdered an Egyptian. It was a complete fiasco, and Moses had to run for his life. He settled down in Midian, with the life of political agitation behind him. He now has a wife and a successful business. He's living the quiet, rural life that people of all times have craved as a peaceful oasis. He's got his order. He's in control of his existence.

And along comes the Lord God. He introduces tension—a burning bush, that talks no less—and brings Moses to a crisis, calling him to a life that will be anything but peaceful and orderly. And about the only thing he can promise Moses is that he will be with him.

What Moses discovers in the course of his life, and what we discover in the course of ours, is that God's presence is enough. The call to be a liberating presence in the world is a demanding one, so demanding as to intimidate the likes of Moses. But Moses's call is our call, and our call is Moses's call, because such is the call of all who give their lives in obedience to Jesus the Liberator, the one who came "to set at liberty those who are oppressed" (Luke 4:18).

To principalities and powers clutching desperately to oppressive order and excessive control, liberation begins with holy chaos.

11

THE LIFE OF FREEDOM

Before we move on, I need to clarify two more things. First, freedom is not merely an add-on, an interesting metaphor, a helpful way of thinking about things, but is intrinsic to the Christian life. Second, I need to explain the freedom we are invited to experience and invite others to know. I've tried to show how freedom plays out in the biblical narrative, but if we don't grasp both of these things—the centrality of freedom and its practical import—we'll become bored with and oppressed by the work of liberation as quickly as we are with mere religion.

First: the centrality of freedom in the Christian life. The Christian faith hinges on two words. One of those words, of course, is *love*.

We live in a world driven by reasons. Not reason, but reasons. We can't imagine doing anything significant unless there is a good reason to do it. But there is one thing we've been shown has no reason: God's love for us. It is not our worthiness or something we've done but the reasonless love of God that is extolled in Scripture time and again, like this:

> Have mercy on me, O God,
>> *according to your steadfast love;*
> according to your abundant mercy
>> blot out my transgressions. (Ps. 51:1, emphasis added)

And this:

> Help me, O LORD my God!
> Save me *according to your steadfast love!*
> (Ps. 109:26, emphasis added)

And of course,

> But God, being rich in mercy, *because of the great love with which he loved us,* even when we were dead in our trespasses, made us alive together with Christ—by grace you have been saved. (Eph. 2:4–5, emphasis added)

Note how the Bible repeatedly chalks up God's love not to any intrinsic worth or value or potential in us; it's not anything we've done that prompts God's love. He loves "according to" his love. It's circular reasoning, unless we see it for what it is: an in-spite-of love. It is the love that protects the man and the woman from the unrelenting consequences of their sin. The love that shows extraordinary patience with that control freak Abraham. The love that time and again seeks the liberation of a people bent on mere control. The love that goes to the cross that we might have life.

This is love without reason—or a "great love." God's love is not compelled by anything we are or do; it is in the purest sense free love, uncoerced love.

Now we come to the second crucial word: *faith.* Sometimes we are tempted to think of faith as something we do, but in fact we bring nothing to the foot of the cross, not even our faith—as if it were something *we* manufactured in our hearts and heads. Nor is faith an *attitude* we create in our breast to show God we really mean it. Faith is not mere intellectual *assent* to prove to God we are thinking soundly. Faith is not even a repentant and contrite heart that works to impress God with our humility. Instead, faith is the unexpected realization that we are condemned criminals, blindfolded and standing before a firing squad, when suddenly we are pardoned. Faith is the surprising apprehension that we can walk out of the prison of spiritual oppression and that we are irrevocably free from all that held us in bondage.

Faith is accepting the fact that there are no conditions, no bargains to be made, no back room deals; that grace is a gift with no strings attached. No strings before and no strings after! Faith is the realization that grace is utterly free.

What we discover in God is that love is not love in the deepest sense if it is motivated by anything intrinsic in the beloved. If our actions are motivated by inherent worth, it is not love. God would be merely giving us our due. Or we would be merely giving others their due, being obligated by some value in them to honor and respect them. Love is not love unless freely given, given for no reason at all but merely out of "great love."

To be clear: this does not mean we are worthless, as some strains of Christian faith have supposed. Indeed we have tremendous worth as beings created and loved by God. But the order is crucial: we have worth because God freely loves us.

The free gift of grace must remain *free*, in fact, if we are going to become the people God calls us to become—people who bask in the liberating gospel and share the liberating gospel with others. If the gospel is in any way, shape, or form a deal, a quid pro quo, a bargain, a contract, then we will always be *obligated* to do our part. It would then be our *duty* to do what God says. It would turn Christian ethics—even

100

the work of liberation—into another *law*, and therefore into another oppressive burden.

God is not looking for people to do their duty, not even the duty of liberation. He's looking for people who will love— love God and neighbor. And love, as defined by God's action toward us, is not coerced by anything outside itself. Love in the deepest sense is always "great love," free love, uncoerced love, given according to love and no other reason.

Thus our call to join Jesus in his liberating work is not merely one way to look at the life of faith. Freedom is found only in faith, and faith is found only in freedom. Faith is our basking in the free grace of God, returning thanks to him with our free obedience, and living and spreading—in word and deed—the life of uncoerced love.

So what does this freedom consist of? Again, two words are of crucial importance. The first is *obedience*.

It's at this point that many shake their heads in puzzlement. That's understandable, because we normally associate the word *obedience* with slavery and coercion. That's because we typically think of *freedom* as that condition that permits us to do whatever we want to do, to be in complete control of our lives. In the normal course of affairs, obedience is giving up what we want to do (that is, our "freedom") in order to do something that someone else wants us to do (obedience).

What we discover in the gospel, however, turns these ideas completely on their heads. That's because the Christian faith wants to deal with life as it really is, not as we imagine it.

To begin with, the Bible assumes that when we do what we want to do—such as when we try to control our lives— we quickly find that we're enslaved. As we've noted, Adam and Eve wanted this type of freedom, and all they got was oppression. This in turn devolved into political, moral, and religious oppression—all of which is crystallized in spiritual oppression. No one put it better than Paul. In

101

this passage, he is speaking to Jews, but the point applies to anyone who strives to live, and help others live, moral and just lives:

> If you are sure that you yourself are a guide to the blind, a light to those who are in darkness, an instructor of the foolish, a teacher of children, having in the law the embodiment of knowledge and truth—you then who teach others, do you not teach yourself? While you preach against stealing, do you steal? You who say that one must not commit adultery, do you commit adultery? You who abhor idols, do you rob temples? You who boast in the law dishonor God by breaking the law. (Rom. 2:19–23)

The point is simple: we find ourselves unable to actually live in a way that is consistent with the ideals we proclaim. Later in the same letter to the Romans, Paul puts it this way:

> I do not understand my own actions. For I do not do what I want, but I do the very thing I hate. . . . For I have the desire to do what is right, but not the ability to carry it out. . . . So I find it to be a law that when I want to do right, evil lies close at hand. For I delight in the law of God, in my inner being, but I see in my members another law waging war against the law of my mind and making me captive to the law of sin that dwells in my members. (7:15, 18, 21–23)

Here and elsewhere, Paul reminds us that when it comes to the most important things—doing those things that lead to truth, beauty, and goodness—we find ourselves bound. We cannot consistently do anything we really want to do, and our best efforts usually undermine our deepest desires. This is the witness of human history, with all those unintended consequences, generation after generation. Add to that our utter inability to change our ultimate fate, death—we simply cannot will to live forever. This is hardly a definition of freedom! It gets to the core of the human dilemma, and it's what caused Paul to cry out: "Wretched man that I am! Who will deliver me from this body of death?" (7:24).

If Paul is the great exegete of the human condition, he is also the great prophet of freedom:

> There is therefore now no condemnation for those who are in Christ Jesus. For the law of the Spirit of life has set you free in Christ Jesus from the law of sin and death. (8:1–2)

This new freedom consists of two things. First is freedom from death and for life:

> If the Spirit of him who raised Jesus from the dead dwells in you, he who raised Christ Jesus from the dead will also give life to your mortal bodies through his Spirit who dwells in you. (8:11)

Now, for the first time, we have a real choice. If we continue in our present existence, denying the redemptive presence of the Spirit, it leads to death. Or we can accept and acknowledge the redemptive work of the Spirit, and thus enjoy an existence that is characterized by everlasting life.

But this new freedom is not about pie in the sky by and by, a promise of hope in the face of death. It is a freedom to begin living today the life we instinctively yearn to live:

> God has done what the law, weakened by the flesh, could not do. By sending his own Son in the likeness of sinful flesh and for sin, he condemned sin in the flesh, in order that the righteous requirement of the law might be fulfilled in us, who walk not according to the flesh but according to the Spirit. (8:3–4)

Still, we remain confused. We often don't know what we *really* want. Our hearts are filled with all types of desires, so many it is hard to sort them out. We have desires for love and for lust, for enjoying the fruit of our labor and for mere money, for security and for mere safety, for justice and for self-interest. If we were left to discern our own hearts and motives, we would remain in a sorry state of subjective confusion, apt to call evil good and good evil. How do we know what we really want, what will really make us happy, what will really make us human, what will really lead to a life of freedom?

We may not know, but of course *God* does. He is the one who fashioned us, who knows better than anyone how he has created us to live. He is the one who chose us before the foundation of the world to be the people he has called us to be. He is the one who set this whole thing up and providentially watched over it—from creation to fall to exodus to exile to the coming of Jesus Christ and the Holy Spirit. He is the one who injected chaos into life from the beginning—that we might learn, slowly but surely, to let go of our addiction to control; that we might slowly but surely grow up in Christ and learn to live in the freedom and love he calls us into.

In particular, God reveals what our freedom looks like in his commands. God never commands us to do anything but that which will help us to become the people we were created to be. The God who created us and died for us, the God who chose to love us before we even came into existence and will love us in an existence that will never end, has no intention toward us other than our good. Thus every command that proceeds from the mouth of God is a word of love.

So when we obey God, we are—finally—able to know and do those things that we have up to now been unable to do: the very things that make life true, good, and beautiful. In this regard, our freedom consists of two things. To begin with, for the first time we are able to hear the command of God as a *gracious* command! Before Christ, we could only hear it as a burden; we did not have the ability—the freedom—to hear it as a mercy. Second, because the Spirit of Jesus lives within us, we have the ability to actually obey the command, that is, to do the thing that we were designed to do, to become the people we were designed to become.

For the Christian, then, obedience is freedom and freedom is obedience.

We began this chapter by talking about the centrality of love, and so we must conclude it. Freedom is not some abstract concept about the ability of the human will. It is nothing less than a way to talk about love. When writing about love, I'm often tempted to add an adjective to it and talk about *uncoerced* love. True love is always uncoerced, always freely given. But we live in an age in which love is often construed as an obligation or a quid pro quo. We love our spouses because they love us. Or we are required to love the poor. And so forth. I want to add the word *uncoerced* not to suggest that love can be coerced but to emphasize this essential attribute of love.

Love is always free, and when one finds freedom, one will find love. God's love for us is uncoerced and so freely given that it does not *demand* a response. But so freely is it given that it creates freedom in the recipient, so that our response is not one of obligation or duty, nor the returning of a favor, but uncoerced love.

The word the Bible often uses for our response of uncoerced love is *thanksgiving*. Paul says that as "grace extends to more and more people" it will "increase thanksgiving, to the glory of God" (2 Cor. 4:15). Thanksgiving is a word, and a tone, that characterizes all of Paul's letters.

So the synonyms expand: to live in thanksgiving to God is to live in uncoerced love toward him (in obedience) and toward others (in service). There we go again, another seeming antonym (*freedom* versus *service*) that in Christ amounts to the same thing. But once we grasp that freedom and obedience and service are all grounded in the same thing—uncoerced love—it will make perfect sense.

12

FROM THE HORIZONTAL TO THE VERTICAL

In this part of this book I want to look at our contemporary situation, at ourselves as individual believers and as members of Jesus's church. I want to suggest how in various ways we subtly turn the gospel of liberation into a religion of control. More importantly, I want to suggest ways in which I believe the Spirit is calling us back into a life of freedom. I can think of no better way to suggest the startling contrast between what we are tempted to become and what we can be than by looking at how the Holy Spirit shaped the early church in the book of Acts.

For instance, one of the most startling things about the preaching found in the book of Acts is how little interest the apostles show in meeting people's needs. Not one sermon by Peter or Paul or Stephen starts off by articulating a felt need of the listeners. Few preachers today would dare begin a sermon without first talking about what listeners are feeling or thinking or wrestling with. But the apostles seem indifferent to their listeners' life situation.

Nor in Acts do we find sermons about how to have a better marriage, how to raise Christian kids, or how to be a better Christian at work. No preaching on how to share your faith or how to change the culture. No jokes. No come-ons. No cute stories about one's kids or wife or what the preacher did on his vacation. The early church did none of these things to win a hearing.

Instead early preachers talked about the story of the Jewish people, interpreted from the perspective of the recently murdered Jesus. They talked about the suffering, death, and resurrection of Jesus, followed by a call to repent. For example, note the end of Peter's first sermon, which summarizes these themes:

> Brothers, I may say to you with confidence about the patriarch David that he both died and was buried, and his tomb is with us to this day. Being therefore a prophet, and knowing that God had sworn with an oath to him that he would set one of his descendants on his throne, he foresaw and spoke about the resurrection of the Christ, that he was not abandoned to Hades, nor did his flesh see corruption. This Jesus God raised up, and of that we all are witnesses. Being therefore exalted at the right hand of God, and having received from the Father the promise of the Holy Spirit, he has poured out this that you yourselves are seeing and hearing. . . . Let all the house of Israel therefore know for certain that God has made him both Lord and Christ, this Jesus whom you crucified. (Acts 2:29–33, 36)

While the call to repent is a regular feature in the apostles' sermons, the spiritual needs or wants of the listeners is never the focus. It's not about their fulfillment or their duty. It's not about their calling or destiny. The sermons are about Jesus Christ.

This is such a contrast to the preaching and outreach in North America in the twenty-first century.

A few years ago, I received a flyer in the mail:

A new flavor of church is in town! Whether you prefer church with a more traditional blend or a robust contemporary flavor, at [church name], we have a style just for you! Casual atmosphere, relevant messages, great music, dynamic kids' programs, and yes, you can choose your own flavor!

The "flavors" were described with phrases intended to attract the unchurched: "Real-life messages," "Safe and fun children's program," "Friendly people," and the coup de grace, "Fresh coffee and doughnuts!"

What pagan could resist? In our better moments, we recall that it is the gospel of Jesus Christ that changes the world. But we often find ourselves practicing the theology of one character in Flannery O'Connor's *Wise Blood*, who said, "If you want to get anywheres in religion, you got to keep it sweet."[1]

There are various ways that we "keep it sweet"—that is, try to make the gospel inviting to as many as possible. We do that usually by focusing on what religion will do for us, or by thinking that the sum and substance of religion is what we do for God. This tendency has created a Christianity that, from the perspective of the book of Acts, is a strange sight indeed.

Sociologist of religion Wade Clark Roof, in his *Spiritual Marketplace: Baby Boomers and the Remaking of American Religion*, described Christianity in the United States like this: "the drift over time, and still today, is in the direction of enhanced choices for individuals and toward a deeply personal, subjective understanding of faith and well-being."[2]

When he focused on evangelicals in particular, he made the same point: "Evidence that the appeal of popular evangelicalism lies primarily in its attention to personal needs, and not dogma or even strict morality, is supported by careful analysis of national surveys. Psychological categories like 'self,' 'fulfillment,' 'individuality,' 'journey,' 'walk,' and 'growth' are all very prominent within evangelical Christianity."[3]

Many other studies say the same thing, but the most important is Christian Smith and Melinda Lundquist Denton's *Soul Searching: The Religious and Spiritual Lives of American Teenagers*. Published in 2005, it is already a classic.[4]

Smith and Denton conducted extensive interviews with 267 American teenagers and concluded that a new religion has emerged in America whose chief tenets are as follows:

- A God exists who created and orders the world and watches over human life on earth.
- God wants people to be good, nice, and fair to each other, as taught in the Bible and by most world religions.
- The central goal of life is to be happy and to feel good about oneself.
- God does not need to be particularly involved in one's life except when God is needed to resolve a problem.
- Good people go to heaven when they die.

Smith and Denton noticed that this "de facto creed" is particularly evident among mainline Protestant and Catholic teenagers "but is also visible among black and conservative Protestants."[5]

Since the authors found that this faith is learned from parents, they conclude, "We have come with some confidence to believe that a significant part of Christianity in the United States is actually only tenuously Christian in any sense that is seriously connected to the actual historical Christian tradition, but has rather substantially morphed into Christianity's misbegotten step-cousin, Christian Moralistic Therapeutic Deism."[6]

This analysis resonates deeply with those familiar with American Christianity. While Smith and Denton intended to describe the state of teenage faith, they seem to have described the faith of many adults as well. The faith of American Christians focuses on the horizontal—on the needs and aspirations of people.

Though this characteristic has become intensified in our therapeutic age, it is not a new development. After his visit to America from late 1831 to early 1832, Alexis de Tocqueville described in eerily contemporary terms two features of American life and the religious tension they produced. While extolling the American emphases on freedom and equality, he said:

> It must be acknowledged that equality, which brings great benefits into the world, nevertheless suggests to men . . . some very dangerous propensities. *It tends to isolate them from each other*, to concentrate every man's attention upon himself; *and it lays open the soul to an inordinate love of material gratification.*[7]

Tocqueville had the prescience to see the individualism and consumerism that would ever plague American Christianity. But he seems to have had an unwarranted confidence in American religion's ability to resist these temptations.

While we hear a variety of critiques and solutions to this problem, we find it almost impossible to talk about the faith as did the early apostles. We keep getting stuck in the horizontal level, even when we are seemingly trying to get people to look up!

Take for example the spiritual formation movement. One of the most promising developments in the church has been the reemergence of spiritual formation, with its emphasis on practices that discipline mind and body so as to open ourselves to the transforming work of the Holy Spirit. Thanks to the pioneering work of Richard Foster and Dallas Willard, the movement has given shape and purpose to the lives of countless evangelicals, saving them from an indolent Christian existence.

The resurgence of interest in the spiritual disciplines began well enough with a strong focus on the vertical. Take Dallas Willard's now classic *The Spirit of the Disciplines: Understanding How God Changes Lives*. The title is a play on words and suggests that the disciplines are a gift of the Holy Spirit. The subtitle clearly states that the book is about understanding *God's* ways.

But note the shift in emphasis as the genre has developed, with book titles and subtitles that highlight the spiritual disciplines' horizontal value. They are about the means for "arranging our lives for spiritual transformation" or for "practices that transform us." One group recently issued a call for Christians to take spiritual formation more seriously. All in all, it's a positive move. Unfortunately it begins with a paragraph that features the first person plural eleven times: "God calls *us* . . . *We* experience . . . This lifelong transformation within and among *us* . . . *We* are called . . . *We* do not always . . ."

To be fair, it is indeed impossible to talk about God without talking about the people he has created and revealed himself to. We only know God in his relation to us. And it should be noted that the second paragraph of the call to spiritual formation highlights the vertical dimension. But what is being communicated if it comes second?[8]

The authors of such books and statements will, in a heartbeat, insist on the divine, gracious nature of the spiritual life. I'm not questioning anyone's theology or motives. I'm only suggesting that such an emphasis, even if we fall into it inadvertently, will eventually have an effect. If we continually put the horizontal first, spiritual formation will, as it has in other ages, morph into an oppressive human religion.

Or take the efforts of the socially concerned. We can never be too thankful for late twentieth-century pioneers in this movement, like Carl Henry, Jim Wallis, and Ron Sider, for calling the church back to this crucial dimension of the Christian life. The renewal of social concern has turned many Christians and churches from a selfish spirituality to a faith characterized by justice and mercy.

I've been following the movement for three decades now—I was an early subscriber to *Sojourners* and the now-defunct *The Other Side*—and in my experience it has been the rare social justice appeal that grounds itself in the gospel of grace, in the cross and resurrection, in the miraculous gift of forgiveness, and in the immense gratitude that naturally flows from that gift.

This relative absence of the vertical—the redeeming work of God in Christ—in social justice rhetoric is matched by a focus on the horizontal. The rhetoric usually assumes that the problem is a lack of human will and that the job of the movement's leaders is to cajole people out of social indifference with whatever psychological tactic is at hand:

- Guilt: Look at others' poverty in comparison to our wealth.
- Fear: What will our world be like if we don't do something about *x* now?
- Shame: How can we call ourselves disciples of Christ and not do *x*?
- Moralism: Exhortations littered with *should*, *ought*, *do*, and *must*.

Sometimes the appeal is less oppressive but nonetheless optimistic about the human will. A recently developed curriculum designed to help churches love their neighbors—specifically in terms of social concern and social justice—used this line in an email marketing piece: "For most of us caught up in the hectic demands on our lives, the biggest problem is not desiring to be the Good Samaritan—it's acting on that desire! It's starting!"

One final example comes from those who attempt to get us out of ourselves by focusing on "the other," meaning people of other races, ethnicities, and cultures. We're still figuring out what a multiethnic Christianity looks like, but no one is arguing anymore that we shouldn't figure it out! For this we can thank not only America's changing demographics but also the prophetic voices and examples of men like John Perkins and Rudy Carrasco.

Yet here too we see a constant horizontal temptation. A leading Asian evangelical recently released a book that seeks to "free the evangelical church from Western cultural captivity." He begins with what everyone recognizes as entrenched problems: our individualism, consumerism, materialism, racism, and cultural imperialism.

But while acknowledging how firmly enslaved we are, the author repeatedly says things like, "Lessons from the black church or lessons arising out of the theology of suffering can lead to freedom from the Western, white captivity of the church."[9] And in an interview to publicize the book, he said, "In fact, the more diverse we become, Christianity will flourish."

The assumptions seem to be these: The church will flourish if we become diverse. The church will become liberated from its cultural captivity if we learn lessons from others. In short, the health of the church depends on what we do. In my personal correspondence with the author about his book, he denied this, and I have no reason to doubt him. But like many of us, he was able to write and publish this book without noting the incongruity. Missing here and in many such worthy efforts is an emphasis on God's power, not human example, to free us from the principalities and powers, and an emphasis on the good news that we are not the ones who must build the *shalom* community but the ones who receive it as gift and promise.

The same horizontal temptations face any one of us who seeks to directly or indirectly reform evangelicalism. A subtitle to a recent book by Ron Sider says a lot about what motivates many of us: *Why Are Christians Living Just Like the Rest of the World?* Similarly, a website that crystallizes the theology and goal of what I call the "following Jesus movement" says, "Following Jesus is about listening and doing. It is about putting into practice the things that Jesus taught. It is about a *lifestyle* of peace and justice *that sets one apart from others*" (emphasis added).[10]

In our righteous frustration lies a temptation that entices us when we start anxiously comparing ourselves with "the rest of the world." This is the temptation of the devout that Jesus described, of the evangelical Pharisee who thanked God that he was no longer like sinners!

We might do better to shift the comparison: the scandal is not that we are just like other people but that we are not more like Jesus.

Other examples abound of our temptation to see only the horizontal. Take the missional movement—again, a crucial corrective for churches that have become nothing more than religious social clubs. It is a corrective that, in its better moments, focuses on the mission of *God*. Yet how easily the conversation slides into what *we* are doing. In an article in which he tried to clarify the nature and purpose of the missional church movement, Brian McLaren defined it as *"an attempt by Western Christians to reclaim our identity* as disciples—people learning to be like Jesus and ready to follow him into our world" (emphasis added).[11]

To be sure, a book title or single remark cannot be used to indict a person or whole sub-movement. Each reform group within evangelicalism has vocal advocates who, while recognizing God's call to move into the horizontal, nonetheless thoroughly ground themselves in the vertical. Yet the overall impression one gets from self-critiques and studies by sociologists of religion is that we are increasingly uninterested in things vertical. As Wade Clark Roof noted in his study, "the 'weightlessness' of contemporary belief in God is a reality . . . for religious liberals and many evangelicals."[12]

114

We're addicted to the horizontal for many reasons, but one is that the horizontal is something we can control. To emphasize what *we* should do puts us in charge of our religion. You start making religion about what God has done and is doing, and you may have to wait around for him to do something. That will never do when you have a religious establishment to run or a mission to accomplish. You've got to give people something to do, or they'll get bored.

I recently heard a preacher succumb to this temptation, which is so easy to do. He was preaching on the classic text Ephesians 6:10–18, a passage that is generally talked about in terms of "spiritual warfare." As so often happens, he focused on all the things we are supposed to do: "put on," "take up," "stand," and so forth. So he spent the bulk of the sermon talking about our spiritual experience and response.

He failed to highlight the fact that Paul begins his discussion like this: "Be strong *in the Lord and in the strength of his might*" (v. 10), which sets the tone for all that follows. Nor did he focus on that which we are to put on: truth, righteousness, the gospel, faith, and salvation. These are not things we manipulate with our actions but *gifts* we receive. A careful reading of this passage shows that it is not primarily about "spiritual warfare" that we are engaged in but is mostly about a battle that has already been won by Another, and the spiritual armor that he provides.

The preacher finally recognized this with his last point: He said that 97 percent of Scripture concentrates on the power of Christ over evil, and he rightly admonished us to fix our gaze there. The irony, of course, is that 97 percent of the sermon was fixed on us and what we do.

This type of Christianity is practical and effective, but in the long run, it becomes oppressive. A religion that points to what we do is a religion that eventually succumbs to legalism or becomes mere duty. The paradox plays itself out: we imagine that by taking control of our faith by emphasizing what we do, we are exercising freedom. In fact, we only become addicted to the horizontal, which in turn only enslaves us to its demands.

The early apostles understood this instinctively, and thus their emphasis on the vertical—on what God has done in Jesus Christ. They didn't ignore the horizontal. Almost every sermon in the book of Acts concludes with an exhortation to repent. But clearly their focus lay elsewhere.

One reason we focus on the horizontal is that we can better predict the results of our preaching and church programs. We conclude with four steps to creating a better marriage, or tell people to bring supplies for the food closet, or have them invite a friend to church. Simple, predictable, and fully within our control.

When you start emphasizing God and what he has done and will do, well, no telling what will happen. After Peter's first sermon, "those who received his word were baptized, and there were added that day about three thousand souls" (Acts 2:41). People start crowding into church, and before you know it, you can't find a parking spot and your favorite pew is taken by some stranger.

Then again, note the result of Peter's second sermon:

> And as they were speaking to the people, the priests and the captain of the temple and the Sadducees came upon them, greatly annoyed because they were teaching the people and proclaiming in Jesus the resurrection from the dead. And they arrested them. (Acts 4:1–3)

Socially important and powerful people may start questioning your relevance, which is another way of saying your sanity. And if they can't lock you in jail, they may lock you out of their lives.

Or take this response to deacon Stephen's sermon: "But they cried out with a loud voice and stopped their ears and rushed together at him. Then they cast him out of the city and stoned him" (Acts 7:57–58). You start putting the emphasis on who Jesus is and what he is about, and you may be driven from your church.

This did not deter the early apostles in the least. They knew what Martin Luther would discover: "One thing, and only one thing, is necessary for Christian life, righteousness, and freedom. That one thing is the most holy Word of God, the gospel of Christ."[13]

The first thing to do when we confront the dysfunctional horizontal, then, is not to address it as if it were a horizontal problem. For those addicted to order and control, that's the temptation—more order and control! No, the way forward is first to release the desire for order and control, to recognize that the main symbol of our faith is not a man swinging a hammer but a man hanging on a cross. In Christ we see complete abandonment of the need to accomplish something useful for God and a forsaking of the self for God and his purposes. The cross, then, is the sign of freedom from the fever of the horizontal.

The paradox, of course, is that dying to the horizontal is precisely the act that brings energy and grace to the horizontal. It is never an either-or, either horizontal or vertical. They can no more be separated than can the sun's light and heat. But heat without light becomes a dark and oppressive hothouse, in which our work for the Lord is nothing but dreary toil. Add sunlight in the open air, and suddenly we find ourselves in the midst of a beautiful summer day. Then even work feels like play, and the children of God once again till the garden in freedom and joy.

13

FROM JUSTICE TO GRACE

The day started normally enough. Peter and John were walking to the temple to pray. This was apparently something they did every day, the type of thing religious people from time immemorial have done. Peter and John then stepped through the Beautiful Gate to enter the temple area and passed a few beggars, as they did every day. And most of these beggars, either by sign or word, pleaded for some money.

This is a reasonable thing for a beggar to do. And the reasonable expectation is that religious people will feel compassion and toss the beggar a few coins.

We don't know what Peter and John usually did in this situation. One might suppose that like us, they sometimes ignored the beggars and sometimes gave up some spare change. But this time, Peter sensed a shift in the wind, the arrival of the Spirit, signaling that some holy chaos was about to be unleashed.

He told the beggar he had no money, but he could give him this: "In the name of Jesus Christ of Nazareth, rise up and walk!" (Acts 3:6).

One can easily imagine a snicker coming from bystanders. Or maybe the lame man sarcastically thinking, *Right. How about just a few coins, mister?*

Peter acted as if what he said was perfectly sensible, and he grabbed the man's hand and pulled him up off the ground. The man's feet and ankles were "made strong" (v. 7) in the very act of Peter pulling him up, so that the man now leaped up and walked with Peter and John into the temple.

This became no ordinary prayer meeting: the man was alternately "walking and leaping and praising God" (v. 8) and clinging to Peter and John. Pandemonium broke out as people watching the man "walking and praising God" now were "filled with wonder and amazement at what had happened" (vv. 9–10). So "utterly astounded" were they, they also ran with Peter, John, and the healed man to Solomon's portico (v. 11).

It was another one of those moments when the Holy Spirit turned reasonable religion—with its mundane expectations for piety and morality—into something extraordinary. We tend to focus on the miraculous as if it were an end in itself— "Wasn't that incredible!"—as if miracles are performed for our spiritual entertainment. No, these moments are signs that point to the extraordinary stuff we live with every day.

A few years ago, the papers were reporting what on the surface sounded like a healthy company rewarding its best and brightest. Over four hundred employees were to receive bonuses. Three-fourths got more than $100,000. Fifty-one received $1 to $2 million; fifteen received more than $2 million; and six received $4 million. The highest bonus stood at $6.4 million.

Bonuses.

That's on top of a salary that was no doubt decent to begin with, given the size of the company. But, hey, this is capitalism. And you reward people for raising the bottom line.

Except these bonuses were handed out to executives of a company on the verge of collapse, one losing more money in three months—$62 billion in the last quarter of 2008 alone—than most of us would see in three thousand lifetimes. These bonuses were given in a company whose financial troubles not only inflicted pain and distress on millions of investors but also threatened to take down a significant portion of the US economy.

I don't comprehend exactly what AIG, the insurance behemoth, did to itself and thus to the rest of us. Something about "credit default swaps" and "exotic derivatives." No matter the explanation, everyone seemed to agree that AIG executives made foolish decisions and the company had no one but itself to blame for its collapse. As Edward M. Liddy, the government-appointed chairman and chief executive of AIG, put it, the company had made mistakes "on a scale few could have ever imagined possible." Who can understand it?

Some argued that if AIG went down, a lot of other companies would fall like dominoes, and many more innocent investors would suffer. The government was justified in infusing the company with cash. Maybe, maybe not. But when Americans heard that some of that money, $165 million, had been used to pay out *bonuses* to executives who got us into a financial crisis in the first place, well, this news didn't sit well. Those who read the news closely said these were not performance bonuses but retention bonuses, incentives to keep talented people on board a sinking business. But the distinction was lost on most of us.

President Obama said it made him angry. Comedian Stephen Colbert said he wanted to lead a pitchfork-wielding mob after the execs. Senator Chuck Grassley of Iowa said the executives should fall on their swords. Representative Paul Hodes of New Hampshire said the initials AIG should stand for "arrogance, incompetence, and greed." Most of us were mad as Hades and weren't going to take it anymore. It was a scandal, a national folly, and we wanted our money back.[1]

In short order, many of these execs were convinced to give some or all of the bonus money back, and the scandal came to an end. Most Americans sighed in relief, because most had no way to process the incomprehensible unfairness of it all.

Yet in a strange way, the incident reminded me of something the church should feel instinctively. As the Bible never tires of reminding us, we are people "filled with all manner of unrighteousness, evil, covetousness, malice. [We] are full of envy, murder, strife, deceit, maliciousness. [We] are . . . foolish, faithless, heartless, ruthless" (Rom. 1:29, 31). The human heart, said the prophet Jeremiah, "is deceitful above all things, and desperately sick; who can understand it?" (Jer. 17:9). You know, the sort of qualities that describe the leaders of AIG—from foolish to ruthless to desperately deceitful. What's surprising is that the Bible describes a God who *seems* to reward this sort of behavior. To paraphrase a famous passage of Paul (see Rom. 5:15–16):

> The free bonus is not like the trespass. For if many died through one man's trespass, much more have the grace of God and the free bonus by the grace of that one man Jesus Christ abounded for many. And the free bonus is not like the result of that one man's sin. For the judgment following one trespass brought condemnation, but the free bonus following many trespasses brought justification.

And more to the point, "God shows his love for us in that *while* we were still sinners, Christ died for us" (Rom. 5:8, emphasis added).

Reasonable religion is one that punishes sin and rewards good behavior. This is so expected that when we preach this religion and live by it in our fellowships, outsiders are not so much intrigued as bored. *Of course*, they think, *that's what religious people are supposed to do.*

If we believed what the gospel actually says—that the unrighteous are treated as if they are righteous—wouldn't some of our listeners be as scandalized as we all were by the AIG bonuses? The very people who have brought a busload of problems on themselves and the planet (for the sins of the parents are visited not only on the children but on the neighbors as well) are the very people who are offered the bonus of redemptive grace. It's a mercy enough that the likes of us—foolish, faithless, heartless, ruthless—should receive the salary of common grace. But now a bonus of saving grace is offered to those who have made mistakes "on a scale few could have ever imagined possible." Who can understand it?

We don't, apparently, which is why we always are trying to turn extraordinary grace into reasonable religion. Reasonable religion is something orderly, something we can control. It's the mere giving of alms to the crippled soul.

We preach grace, but we also insist that you repeat a little prayer or sign a salvation contract before you can receive the bonus. Or you have to live as if you were on parole; behave yourself long enough, and you'll get a bonus of eternal life. Grace, yes, but you've got to give at least half of it back.

I wonder if we're preaching or living the gospel if we don't scandalize a few listeners, maybe even ourselves, with the incomprehensible unfairness of it all. When Paul talked about the gospel, many were shocked and appalled. It sounded as if God wanted to reward sinners, to give a bonus to scoundrels! They scoffed, "Are we to continue in sin that grace may abound?" (Rom. 6:1). If we start taking grace seriously, pandemonium might break loose, as it did when Peter and John healed the lame man.

We prefer reasonable religion. Take this business of miracles. Reasonable religion has taught us to pray and give alms. Miracles are possible, we formally acknowledge, but then again, we don't like to be disappointed. So our prayers are not so much for divine and miraculous healing but for wisdom for doctors and nurses. Or we just raise money to build clinics.

We do this, of course, because miraculous religion has deservedly gotten a bad name. It may be true that the holy chaos of the Spirit made some miracle possible. Someone prayed for another who was healed, and before you know it, some preacher is exhorting people to claim their miracle. They start pointing to all those verses that seem to imply that the only thing stopping us from more miracles is lack of faith. They hold healing crusades and tell people to "expect a miracle," acting as if the whole business were under our control. That leads inevitably to disappointment by sufferers and the discovery of not a few charlatans. So we run the faith healers out and get control of things again.

But notice: there's not much difference between reasonable religion and miraculous religion. Both are attempts to bring the unexpected work of the Spirit under our control. In the one case, we've made healing the province of our doing—train up doctors and nurses and build clinics. And in the other case, we've made healing the province of our attitudes—have more faith!

If we try to tame miracles, even more so do we try to tame grace. Reasonable religion has taught us not to take grace too seriously. We give a few alms of moralism to silence the desperate cries of the guilty and get on with our prayer meetings. If we were to stop and give people Jesus Christ himself, well, you never know who would start showing up at church—maybe a bunch of crippled human beings. Before you know it, they'll be on the church membership rolls, and then they'll get nominated for the church board. My gosh, who knows what policies they might promote? Or what type of people they'll attract. Pretty soon we'll have to open a homeless shelter and start ministering to prostitutes and drug addicts. We may even have to let a disreputable insurance executive take communion with us.

In fact, when a church starts attracting such people, you can be sure that holy chaos is at work. Most churches are happy with making people a little better. The Holy Spirit comes along and announces that the church's business is helping the lame walk and the blind see and bringing life to the dead.

To be sure, some churches are known for proclaiming grace. But unfortunately for some, grace has become a mere principle. You can tell it's become such when they start using grace to bludgeon people who don't talk about grace the way they do. Some people can get awfully judgmental about grace. Again, notice what is happening. If reasonable religion tries to control grace and rein it in with moralism, the religion of grace tries to control by means of a principle. It justifies all behavior by pulling out the grace card and waving it—and condemning people who don't. It is a principle that we control, and it is this principle that orders our lives.

But biblical grace is not a principle. You cannot have a relationship with a principle. You cannot disappoint a principle. You cannot be forgiven by a principle. You cannot love a principle. You are in control of a principle from start to finish.

Grace is first and foremost a merciful gift of a loving God. This gift is very personal, offered to us each and every time we fail to live as the very personal God has called us to live. Grace is the offer of a very personal forgiveness by a loving heavenly Father who cares deeply about everything we do.

To receive this grace is to know unimaginable freedom— freedom from the colorless expectations of a merely moral life, with its predictable and dreary consequences. Freedom to live as people who, though they have made mistakes "on a scale few could have ever imagined possible," now enjoy a divine bonus that will scandalize and intrigue a confused world.

14

FROM OPTIMISM TO RESURRECTION

The authorities had the hardest time getting the new religion under control. They threw the apostles into jail, and the Holy Spirit liberated them in the middle of the night. The authorities ordered the apostles to stop preaching about Jesus, but the apostles just went right ahead.

It's hard to say what most infuriated the authorities, but you can be sure they were not comforted by talk of the resurrection. In fact, it seems to be the thing that set them off.

Take the encounter in Acts 5. The apostles—which ones exactly is not noted, though Peter is clearly included—had been arrested but were absent from their cells the next morning. Instead, we find Peter and others preaching in the temple area. Given that people were hanging on Peter's every word, the captain and his officers had to be more delicate than usual; still, they somehow manage to convince Peter and others to come before the council.

"We strictly charged you not to teach in this name," says the high priest, "yet here you have filled Jerusalem with your teaching, and you intend to bring this man's blood upon us" (v. 28). In other words, you're not only making the name of Jesus more popular, but you are also pinning the blame for his death on us.

To this Peter replies,

We must obey God rather than men. The God of our fathers raised Jesus, whom you killed by hanging him on a tree. God exalted him at his right hand as Leader and Savior, to give repentance to Israel and forgiveness of sins. And we are witnesses to these things, and so is the Holy Spirit, whom God has given to those who obey him. (vv. 29–32)

So, yes, there's a little insubordination—"We must obey God rather than men" (v. 29). But this isn't what sets off the authorities. And I'm not convinced it is Peter's rather indelicate accusation that they were the ones who had killed Jesus. They knew very well they had had Jesus executed, and frankly, they were not ashamed. Better that one man should die for the nation, as one of them said, than cause problems with Rome.

But when Peter is done, members of the council are "enraged" and want to kill the apostles (v. 33). What is it that sets them off?

I think it is the preaching of the resurrection.

Peter never would have gotten into trouble preaching about the resurrection if he preached it as we do. Peter doesn't use it as a way to talk about new tomorrows. Nothing about good arising from the bad, or how the bare trees of winter turn inevitably into the blossoms of spring, or how we should have hope no matter how bad things get. None of that sentimental stuff for Peter.

Instead he says the resurrection vindicates Jesus's life and death: "The God of our fathers raised Jesus, whom you killed by hanging him on a tree. God exalted him at his right hand as Leader and Savior" (vv. 30–31). In other words, the one you killed as a criminal, God has shown by the resurrection to be Leader and Savior.

Peter makes the same homiletical move in other sermons. On the day of Pentecost, after again blaming the crowd for the crucifixion of Jesus, he says, "Let all the house of Israel therefore know for certain that God has made him both Lord and Christ, this Jesus whom you crucified" (Acts 2:36).

The resurrection is not a sign of sentimental hope but, among other things, a signal that all those who participated in Jesus's death are guilty of that death. Jesus is who he said he was: Lord and Christ. And those who killed him, or cheered on his killing, were wrong.

At Pentecost, the listeners are "cut to the heart," but they at least have the humility to ask, "What shall we do?" (2:37).

Peter's response is, again, not how resurrection preaching is supposed to go. He doesn't say, "We've all made mistakes, but the resurrection shows that God can turn mistakes into opportunities!" No, he says, "Repent!" Admit you were wrong, wrong, wrong. And get baptized—show publicly that you are sorry for what you've done and that you intend to honor Christ as Lord.

To the council, Peter says the same thing: "God exalted him at his right hand as Leader and Savior, to give repentance to Israel. . . . And we are witnesses to these things, and so is the Holy Spirit, whom God has given to those who obey him" (5:31–32).

Indeed, it is a typical sermon of the early church, and like many good sermons, it has three major points:

1. We are the ones who put Christ on the cross. Sometimes the context was the literal officials who really did have Christ nailed to the cross. But as in the Pentecost sermon, the blame is generalized: the logic seems to be that if Christ died for our sins, then we, along with the officials, have crucified Christ.

127

2. The resurrection shows that God has vindicated Christ's life and death. It is God's way of saying Christ is right and you who killed him are wrong.
3. You should repent to receive forgiveness for this and other sins.

In other words, the typical Acts sermon may have been about the resurrection, but it was not a happy Easter sermon so popular today.

⚮

Thirty-five years ago, Ernst Becker began his now-classic *The Denial of Death* with:

> The idea of death, the fear of it, haunts the human animal like nothing else; it is a mainspring of human activity—activity designed largely to avoid the fatality of death, to overcome it by denying in some way that it is the final destiny of man.[1]

It is now commonplace to note the many ways our culture has sidelined death. We live at a frenzied pace and with myriad distractions that keep the thought of death at bay. We fixate on any piece of scientific evidence that suggests that a change in diet or lifestyle might add a year or so to our lives. Graveyards no longer surround churches, nor can they be found at the center of cities, but only at their peripheries. Let the dead lie with the dead.

Enter the resurrection. To be sure, the resurrection is, among other things, the great yes of God to the no of death. But that yes is not as simple or as painless as we are wont to make it. Very often we use the resurrection to deny death rather than live through it to new life.

Often we use resurrection like the grieving use cremation. The rising popularity of cremation is due to many causes, some of them grounded in fine motives, but in many cases it is having a troubling effect. Many who request cremation ask that their ashes be spread in some beautiful, scenic, life-affirming place. We released my father's ashes, for instance, beneath the Golden Gate Bridge in San Francisco Bay. It was a beautiful moment at a beautiful place. We were carrying out my father's wishes, and I thought it a splendid idea at the time, believing that from then on, whenever I might see a picture of the Golden Gate Bridge or visit San Francisco, I would think of my father.

I visited the Bay area a few years later and drove across that magnificent span. While a thought of my father crossed my mind, I can't say it was any more than that. There was too much to distract me. The Golden Gate Bridge is stunning, with those magnificent orange towers rising up, framed by the city skyline and Marin County, overlooking the vast blue expanse of the Pacific Ocean—well, one can think of hardly anything else at such a moment. That setting has a way of making one forget about the dead.

During that same weekend, I visited my mother's crypt, which lies outside of San Francisco. Her remains rest in an unimaginative square building, lined floor to ceiling with shiny marble, a place where every footstep and whisper bounces around for minutes before coming to rest. Mom lies four or five rows up—each row lined with names and dates of demise—and we had to find a ladder to add some fresh flowers to the little vase that is attached to the crypt. For all the sterility of the setting, it has this going for it: there is nothing there to distract one from thinking about the dead.

I found myself crying the whole time I was there—this some twenty-seven years after her death. My sister asked if it was hard for me to be there. No, it wasn't, I replied. But I couldn't pinpoint what I was crying about, because no particular memory of my mother had been stirred up, and I was not feeling an acute sense of loss. My tears, I later concluded, were simply a jumble of ongoing grief and gratitude. Nothing like this could possibly happen at the Golden Gate Bridge.

Sometimes I wonder if Easter has become the Golden Gate Bridge of the church, where we pull out all the stops—importing musical brass and balloons and a greenhouse of lilies, all to create an overwhelming, magnificent effect. This would not be a concern if it weren't for the fact that week by week, we act as if we've cremated death. No more graveyards around the church. No small group Bible studies on how to die well. No spiritual disciplines that focus on our mortality—like the medieval practice of meditating on a skull. No more preaching about our mortality, except as a quick setup for eternal life. No, it's your best life now. We know that if we're going to keep those pews filled, we can't be going on and on about death.

I sometimes wonder whether our churches—living as we do in American death-denying culture, relentlessly smiling through our praise choruses—are inadvertently helping people live not as much in hope as in denial.

"There are, as is known, insects that die in the moment of fertilization," said philosopher Søren Kierkegaard. "So it is with all joy: life's highest, most splendid moment of enjoyment is accompanied by death."[2]

To put it theologically, just as we like to note that Good Friday points to Easter, Easter points back to Good Friday. Easter is not about a giddy happiness that dulls the pain of life, helping us forget our troubles for a day. It can be a triumphant hope, but it is always a sobering hope for those in the midst of a death walk—that is, all of us.

The other way we deny death is willful activity: feverish exercise, Spartan diet, and extraordinary medical care.

The 2009 announcement of the results of yet another diet study is typical: "Daily Red Meat Raises Chances of Dying Early." That got this steak lover's attention. Apparently the

National Institutes of Health got together with the AARP and conducted a diet and health study. They started in 1995 and began following over half a million predominantly white people from the ages of 50 to 71. Not surprisingly, nearly 48,000 men and over 23,000 women died in the following ten years.[3]

What did surprise some was the finding that, taking into account smoking and physical activity, those who ate the most red meat—a quarter of a pound a day—were more likely to die during the study, and most of these died from heart disease and cancer.

Even an amateur scientist can question some of the methods and conclusions of the study (e.g., one can assume that diet and habits and genetics may offer more insight as to why red meat eaters in their later years are susceptible to heart disease). But despite my skepticism, I'll probably eat less red meat than ever!

That study is one of many that have bombarded us for decades. The bottom line is that food of all sorts—but especially food that we have traditionally enjoyed the most, the lusty foods dripping with sweetness and fat—is now seen as a threat.

A threat to what? Longevity. Most of these studies are about discovering the relationship of a food or nutrient to death. Concerns about disease and health are certainly part of the package, but the ultimate goal is to forestall death and extend our days.

This fixation on food's relationship to death is but another sign of our culture's deep fear of death. The subtext of these studies is "Eat and exercise like a Spartan now, and be active and alert into your nineties—and with Viagra, anything is possible!"

This addiction to longevity is especially evident in the area of medical care—*especially* among the most devout.

The *Los Angeles Times* in 2009 reported on a study that showed that "terminally ill cancer patients were nearly three times more likely to go on breathing machines or receive other invasive treatments if religion was an important part of their decision-making process." This was true even though such treatments didn't improve a person's long-term chances.[4]

In other words, it was the most religious who seemed to want to hang on to life the hardest, no matter the prospects. The writer, Karen Kaplan, bent over backwards to be charitable about it, saying, "And for some, extending life by days or even hours buys precious time for prayers to be answered." But it's easy to see that religious people, like everyone else, are desperate to hold on to life as long as possible.

Some rightly argue that we are to be good stewards of our bodies and that even the Bible treats longevity as a blessing. Yes—up to a point. But according to Jesus, part of discipleship is putting our bodies at risk for the gospel. And if Paul was driven by good bodily stewardship, it's hard to imagine why he would have put himself in situations in which shipwrecks, beatings, and hunger were a regular part of the regimen.

Combine a strict regimen of diet and exercise with a healthy dose of resurrection optimism, and you end up with a people who find Paul's attitude toward death nearly unimaginable:

> For to me to live is Christ, and to die is gain. If I am to live in the flesh, that means fruitful labor for me. Yet which I shall choose I cannot tell. I am hard pressed between the two. My desire is to depart and be with Christ, for that is far better. (Phil. 1:21–23)

All this denial, of course, is an attempt to bring order to our lives, which are irrevocably heading toward the great disorder—death. We attempt to control our fear by taking positive action and thinking positive thoughts. Our optimistic Christianity is a religion of attitude—our attitude, fueled by willful, upbeat activity. The resurrection of Jesus seems to fit the bill nicely.

And for good reason. If we have hoped in Christ only in this life, says Paul, we are of all people the most to be pitied. The resurrection is, among other things, the announcement that death has lost its deathly sting. But the resurrection without the crucifixion is empty optimism, an optimism that gives credence to Freud's notion that wishful thinking is the sum and substance of our faith.

Include the crucifixion—and our role in that bloody moment—and the whole picture changes. Now we're not talking about pie in the sky by and by but about an event in history for which we are responsible. We were there when they crucified our Lord, and we were there shouting, "Crucify him!" As theologian Dietrich Bonhoeffer noted, when we meet Christ, either we must die, or he must die.[5] Because we don't want to die to self, our natural instinct is to act like Jesus is the criminal and nail him to the cross, thus pushing him out of our lives.

The resurrection, first and foremost, shows that Jesus is right and we are wrong. He is Lord and we are guilty sinners. To acknowledge this is no small thing, for it means giving up control of one's destiny. It means repenting—turning away from the path we've chosen and following his way. It means giving up the little tricks we use to deny death. It means to face into death with boldness and courage, knowing the terrible thing that it is (a sign of our rebellion against our Creator and our just deserts) *and* that it is not the last word—and not because of our optimism or positive thinking or sentimental thoughts, but because of the power of God.

By God's grace, the Holy Spirit will not leave us mired in sentimentality. Here and there, time and again, the Spirit jolts our lives with sad and vivid reminders that all the optimism in the world cannot change our inevitable destination. It's at those moments, when the prospects seem so bleak, that once again the Spirit cuts us to the heart and we react like the first hearers of the gospel: "What shall we do?"

That's the moment when the chains of mere optimism are broken, when our fear of death and addiction to denial evaporate, when the liberating power of the gospel is made known afresh. Instead of trying to justify and bolster our existence with mere positive thinking, we can acknowledge that what makes this life worth living is that Jesus is right and that he is Lord.

15

FROM MARKETING TO WITNESS

If we were to take this biblical book more seriously, we might have to rename it "The Marketing Blunders of the Apostles."

It's obvious that none of them had taken a marketing class and that none specialized in public relations. Who knows what they might have accomplished if they had? As it is, they made about every marketing mistake possible as they tried to get this new church off the ground.

On the day of Pentecost, Peter has his listeners eating out of his hand. The whole Jerusalem crowd has just witnessed a miracle—people glorifying God in a plethora of languages—and they are curious about from whence this came. Peter begins with a strong rhetorical move, comparing what was happening with something they already held in high respect: their Scriptures. He points out how what is taking place right in front of them matches what the godly prophet Joel wrote about long ago.

But then Peter sticks his foot in his mouth. He starts talking about a notorious criminal, someone who just received the death penalty, killed at the behest of the Jerusalem populace, many of whom were no doubt standing in front of him. And he calls this criminal the "Messiah." This alone sets his sermon back considerably, but then he blames the crowd for killing this man: "This Jesus . . . *you* crucified and killed by the hands of lawless men" (Acts 2:23, emphasis added). Lawless men! Adding insult to injury, he says not this man but the crowd is criminal.

And in case they don't get it, he drives home this indelicate point at the end of the sermon: "Let all the house of Israel [now equated with lawlessness] therefore know for certain that God has made him both Lord and Christ, this Jesus whom *you* crucified" (2:36, emphasis added).

It's no surprise that the Holy Spirit has to take over from here, because this is a public relations disaster. When the Spirit takes over, of course, things start to move in the right direction: "Now when they heard this they were cut to the heart" (2:37). In the end, three thousand people are converted. But who knows what an opportunity Peter missed?

Well, he doesn't, that's for sure. Apparently the apostles did not have a debriefing after this event, as we might today, noting what went well and what could be improved the next time around. We find Peter making the same marketing blunders time and again.

After healing a lame man, Peter again addresses a crowd of people who, again impressed with a miracle, are hanging on his every word. But once more he goes where PR people never dare to tread:

> Men of Israel, why do you wonder at this, or why do you stare at us, as though by our own power or piety we have made him walk? The God of Abraham, the God of Isaac, and the God of Jacob, the God of our fathers, glorified his servant Jesus, whom you delivered over and denied in the presence of

Pilate, when he had decided to release him. But *you denied the Holy and Righteous One*, and asked for a murderer to be granted to you, and *you killed the Author of life*, whom God raised from the dead. To this we are witnesses. (Acts 3:12–15, emphasis added)

He tries to soften the blow by telling them, "Brothers, I know that you acted in ignorance" (3:17), but this likely comes across as patronizing. It's no wonder that the religious leaders are "greatly annoyed." Luke tells us this is because these uneducated laymen are (a) "teaching the people" and (b) "proclaiming in Jesus the resurrection from the dead" (4:2). But it's easy to see that Peter's approach is not helping matters. So they throw Peter and John, his preaching partner, in jail.

Again the Holy Spirit has to take over after these dismal efforts, so that another two thousand join the church.

As I said, Peter is a slow learner. For in other speeches before authorities, he again says, "Let it be known to all of you and to all the people of Israel that by the name of Jesus Christ of Nazareth, whom *you crucified* . . ." and "The God of our fathers raised Jesus, whom *you killed* . . ." (4:10; 5:30, emphasis added). It's no surprise that this rhetorical strategy has this effect: "When they heard this, they were enraged and wanted to kill them" (5:33).

Part of the problem, of course, is that the apostles don't seem much concerned about their reputations or that of the church, as long as they are true to their Lord. At one point, after being beaten and ordered to speak no more about Jesus, "They left the presence of the council, rejoicing that they were counted worthy to suffer dishonor for the name" (5:41).

A marketing consultant would have told them that the point was not to suffer dishonor but to gain honor if they wanted to sell their message to a hostile audience. Clearly the apostles were marketing impaired. We can only thank God that the Holy Spirit was helping out.

Today we think we know better, and we talk a lot about the power of marketing and not as much about the power of the Holy Spirit. This is understandable. The Spirit is wild and unpredictable, and often hard to pin down about what we should do next. Marketing is a proven science of how to get and hold people's attention and create a memorable brand. Marketing has been wildly successful in helping businesses and speakers gain greater followings, no question about it.

The problem with marketing is, again, the illusion it gives us of control. The most egregious example of this was a news release that crossed my desk one day at *Christianity Today*: "Church Check, a division of parent company Guest Check Inc., announced today the immediate availability of a new service offering, widely differing in scope from its current client base within the hospitality industry."

The name "Church Check" naturally caught my attention, as did the offer of the new service. So I read on:

> After years of success focusing only in Hospitality, Guest Check was approached by a single church congregation over two years ago, and was asked to consider providing inspection services. Their primary goal was to assess the Sunday morning experience of a non-biased third party visitor. . . . The church leadership wanted to get an unbiased and anonymous review of the "guest" experience.

For more information, the reader was invited to go to a website, which I did. There I found the idea further explained:

> Our team of savvy professionals can secretly worship at your church, analyze it in detail, and present you with a report detailing items that are lacking. With this report, you can make changes that boost your retention rate and make your church grow. Make the adjustments our team suggests and you'll not only retain more of your first-time visitors, you'll get them talking to their friends about you.

And this:

> Guest Check helps you create an environment in which your
> guests enjoy themselves so much they don't want to leave.
> More importantly, we help you create a church whose guests
> can't stop talking about it, and we all know the power of
> word-of-mouth marketing.

So what do these "church inspectors," as they are called,
bring with them as they assess these churches?

> Regardless of the church's religious affiliation, inspectors
> must be willing to make the visit with an open mind and be
> comfortable assessing your experience on a very objective and
> non-emotional level. Successful Church Check Inspectors are
> professional, attentive, organized and able to express their
> observations objectively and without emotion.

And why, right now, might churches need this service?

> Statistics like this show that more than ever, Americans have
> no problem with church-shopping, or leaving their current
> congregation and moving on to another.

This, thank God, was a short-lived experiment. Guest Check
Inc. no longer offers this service. But the language used to sell
this product has become the common language of so many
churches and ministries that we hardly notice it anymore.

Why would a church—a place that is supposedly characterized by genuineness and humility—ask a group of "savvy
professionals" to help it? Is it possible for "savvy professionals" to understand what a church is really about?

Is worship that is practiced "secretly," with the goal of
"assessing" the "experience on a very objective and non-
emotional level" really *worship* of God Almighty, Creator
of heaven and earth? Can one truly enter into a worshiping community objectively, secretly, and without emotion?

Worship is not about judging the "worship experience" but about putting oneself humbly before God to be judged and forgiven by him.

Furthermore, to enter into the community of God—that is, to grasp the essence of that unique experience—one must come as an identified individual, who is willing to lay his secrets before God and to some degree before others (confessing sins to one another, as James says), who gives himself, body and soul, to the love of God, and who does so with emotional freedom. To try to worship while suppressing these vital and warm human elements is surely to fail to grasp what you are doing.

Should churches make it a goal to "boost your retention rate and make your church grow," or to serve Jesus Christ faithfully? Do churches really want to create an institution "whose guests can't stop talking about" it? Isn't the point of the church to get people thinking and talking about Jesus Christ?

All in all, such language only exacerbates the fundamental and tragic lie that infects the hearts and minds of so many churches and "guests" today: that it is up to us to shape the perceptions of the church, that we're in charge of the church's reputation.

When we "market," we try to make a larger audience aware of the value of a good or service. Paying money for a good or service is the sort of thing that goes on day in and day out in our culture. Both parties benefit from a transaction over which both have some control. It's all very orderly.

Marketing outside the church is a wonderful thing. I like to hear pitches about products I might use. And I have no problem with my publishers marketing my books to a larger public! It is the way our culture makes products and services known.

But there's a reason marketing should be exorcised from the church, why Jesus said, "You shall be my witnesses" and not "You shall be my marketers."

In fact, Jesus seemed to discourage marketing. Take his dramatic healing of a leper, after which he sternly commanded him, "See that you say nothing to anyone" (Mark 1:44). Scholars call this repeated behavior "the messianic secret," and many preachers imagine that Jesus had mostly pragmatic concerns in mind: if word of his power spread, he not only would have been flocked by crowds, but he would also have been prematurely crucified by the authorities.

Maybe. But soft-pedaling the Good News seems intrinsic to its message. Jesus spoke in parables, he said, not to reveal the Good News but to hide it: "For those outside everything is in parables, so that 'they may indeed see but not perceive, and may indeed hear but not understand'" (Mark 4:11–12). Elsewhere he specifically told his disciples not to cast gospel pearls before swine. Make something as cheap as slop, and people will treat it like slop.

Jump ahead twenty centuries, and we find a church that doesn't think twice about treating the gospel like fast food. About thirty years ago, the church growth movement exploded onto the scene; churches became enamored with the efficiency of businesses like Disneyland and McDonald's, and they began fashioning their life to meet people's needs in the same ways—except that their product was the gospel. So churches became places where thousands could be served efficiently. And where the message was served in McSermons, which could be easily digested and applied. And where marketing became the church's first language.

When the church starts marketing itself or the gospel, something odd is taking place. It subtly turns the free gift of grace into a transaction. It harnesses the unpredictable God and shackles him to a transaction. It suggests that the church is offering people some benefit they can consume. At the same time, it inadvertently suggests that the church somehow receives a benefit in return—more warm bodies at its services, for one. When you market the church, the assumptions of the marketplace—that it's all about an *exchange* of value for goods and services—begin to pervade the church.

No wonder, then, that in the era when the church has marketed itself more and more, neighborhoods and cities increasingly see the church as just another business and are increasingly resentful of its presence in their communities. Today churches have a heck of a time trying to get permits for expanding or building because communities think they're a nuisance. To many of these cities, the church exchanges goods and services, albeit spiritual goods and services. And when this becomes the sense of what a church is about, naturally neighborhoods are not keen on being exploited (with traffic, parking problems, and meetings at all hours of the day and night) just to promote the business of the church.

And it's no wonder we find church people more transient than ever. If church is like a business, members will demand more and more from their churches, and if churches don't deliver, people will take their spiritual business elsewhere. Granted, there is something of a chicken and egg problem here. In some respects, churches started marketing themselves like a business to attract fickle people who had begun to think of the church as a spiritual product. But it's also clear to see how churches have only exacerbated the problem by buying into the assumption themselves.

And should it surprise us that in this era, pastors increasingly think of themselves as managers, leaders, and CEOs and that preaching has become less an exposition of the gospel of Jesus's death and resurrection and more often practical lessons that offer a lot of "takeaway *value*," presented in an efficient, friendly manner, as if we were selling cheeseburgers, fries, and a shake?

The problem, again, is not marketing as such or trying to help people know the wonders of the gospel! It's when the means become the ends, when the method becomes a kind of madness, when we subtly imagine that a result—more members in the pews or more money in the offering plate—is dictated by our marketing model. The problem is that a living faith in the dynamic and unpredictable work of the Spirit has turned into a dreary business with predictable results.

This is not freedom but a new legalism, the mere following of rules—albeit the rules of marketing. Pity the poor pastor who, believing he is led by the Spirit, suggests a course of action that risks losing members or money. Pity poor us when, prompted by the Spirit, we think about doing something risky or radically loving, only to hold back because we don't know what it will do to our reputation—that is, our personal brand! To live at the beck and call of marketing logic is to live in slavery.

Instead of trying to manage our reputations or our church brand, how much more freeing would it be simply to point to Jesus as the way, the truth, and the life? Instead of selling faith as a transaction ("Believe in Jesus and you'll benefit in this life and the next!"), wouldn't it be more liberating simply to describe what Jesus has done for us? In short, instead of marketing the faith, wouldn't it be so much easier to be witnesses?

Note how our marketing mentality has infected our ability to share our faith personally with friends. If we don't have a dramatic testimony or polished patter or an effective argument worked up—a prepared marketing presentation!—we feel inadequate. We've come to believe that this sort of thing should be left to professionals, people who know all the techniques of persuasion.

But originally, evangelism was a matter of being a witness—telling people what God has done in your life. We "witness" about many things in our day-to-day lives. We tell others how much we enjoyed an outing at a certain park. Or how much we like a certain book. Or what store we like to shop at. Such witnessing is natural for us. And it is freeing. We don't have to convince people to like a certain book, for example. We just point to it and say that it was meaningful to us in this way and that. And then we encourage them to get a copy of the book, or we lend them our own, and we let the book convince them that it is worth reading. We just point.

Similarly, we are called not to market Jesus to friends, but simply to point to him. We just tell them the difference he has made in our lives. Nothing more, nothing less. And then we let the Spirit demonstrate that Jesus is indeed the way, the truth, and the life, and allow him to touch people's lives with saving grace.

It's a little unnerving when you first start doing this— actually trusting that the Holy Spirit will work in another person's life. The Spirit often does not do it in the way we'd do it, and certainly not on our timetable.

I had a college friend with whom I had many an argument about the faith—all to no effect. And then a few years after we graduated, I received a Christmas card from him, which he signed with "In the name of our Savior." Needless to say, the word *our* caught my attention, and I phoned him. Naturally, I expected to hear that my arguments had finally convinced him. But when I asked him what had prompted him to become a Christian, he said it was the example of his mother. He didn't even mention my persuasive arguments!

Sometimes the Holy Spirit uses the strangest people to prod others into the faith. I have a friend who was fascinated with atheism in college. He found himself drawn to some of the most ardent and skeptical among them, like the French existentialist philosopher Albert Camus. But after spending some time in Camus's novel *The Plague*, he came to a rather unusual conclusion:

> Camus was right, I knew, and I, too, had plague. I was sick and in need of a Physician. Camus' willingness to accept the truth that human beings are fallen allowed me to do the same. Camus held a mirror to my face—in a way that no pastor, preacher, or professor had—and I knew I needed salvation.[1]

"Where the Spirit of the Lord is, there is freedom," says Paul (2 Cor. 3:17). And we are most in line with the Spirit, most faithfully obedient, when instead of trying to manipulate people into faith, we simply live in that freedom and let the Spirit do the work of transformation.

16

FROM MANAGING TO BEING MANAGED

After the stoning of Stephen, Luke tells us in Acts 8, "there arose on that day a great persecution against the church in Jerusalem, and they were all scattered throughout the regions of Judea and Samaria, except the apostles" (v. 1). Here we see more of the chaotic work of the Spirit. He may not have caused the "great persecution," but he certainly made use of it.

First, the Spirit used this seeming setback to further the mission of the church. As Jesus said to the apostles, "You will be my witnesses in Jerusalem and in all Judea and Samaria, and to the end of the earth" (1:8). None of the twelve had yet ventured outside the walls of Jerusalem. Now finally, after seven chapters, we see the church making its way to Samaria: "Now those who were scattered went about preaching the word" (8:4).

Second, the Spirit used the occasion to liberate another deacon. Philip, like Stephen, had been ordained to feed the

Hellenistic widows. One might conclude that if the chief apostles weren't up for the task of going out from Jerusalem, the Holy Spirit would find someone who was—even if he wasn't "qualified." Up to this point, we have no inkling that Philip can preach, but once he found himself pushed out of the Jerusalem nest, without any widows to serve, he naturally would have asked, "Now what?" For whatever reason, he thought he could do street preaching: "Philip went down to the city of Samaria and proclaimed to them the Christ" (8:5).[1] The impact on the city was electrifying:

> And the crowds with one accord paid attention to what was being said by Philip when they heard him and saw the signs that he did. For unclean spirits, crying out with a loud voice, came out of many who had them, and many who were paralyzed or lame were healed. So there was much joy in that city. (8:6–8)

The timing and circumstances could not have been better for Philip to remain in this city indefinitely. It was clear that the Spirit had led him to Samaria, that he had blessed Philip's ministry, that the fields were ripe unto harvest. Time to get organized, time to put some programs into place, time to start a megachurch!

And yet the next time we come across Philip in the book of Acts, we read this: "Now an angel of the Lord said to Philip, 'Rise and go toward the south to the road that goes down from Jerusalem to Gaza.' This is a desert place" (8:26).

Philip was told to move from a city lush with ministry possibilities, where people with deep spiritual needs were welcoming the work of the church, to a desert place, where no one lived.[2] Instead of managing a ministry, Philip was being managed—and he seemed to accept it as a matter of course: "And he rose and went" (8:27).

Such openness to the Spirit is, unfortunately, not as common as it might be.

147

We live in the most managerial, bureaucratic, organized period of the church's history. We might call this the megachurch era. Megachurches are large religious organizations that depend on sophisticated managerial techniques to keep them running efficiently. Many cathedral churches in late antiquity and in the Middle Ages were essentially megachurches, so this isn't a new phenomenon or something essentially evil. But megachurches have been the exception—the vast, vast majority of churches in the long sweep of Christian history have been smaller congregations. While megachurches might still make up a minority of congregations today, they have become the epitome of church life. When many people think of "church" today, as often as not they think of a megachurch.

The megachurch sets the pace and the agenda for churches of all sizes today. In the past, large churches would look to smaller churches as models of the pastoral sensitivity and parish intimacy they longed to retain, despite their size. Today small churches look to megachurches as models and will buy books and DVDs and attend costly seminars thousands of miles away to learn the management principles of these massive churches. It's not the size nor the effectiveness of megachurches that signals a troubling development, but the reliance of churches large and small on managerial thinking as the key to success.

Hardly a week goes by at *Christianity Today* that I don't receive an email that assumes that the answer to the church's problems is better management—of people, of programs, of facilities. That people, programs, and facilities often need better management is something few church members would deny. But notice the language used to promote a recent conference on "Worship Facilities":

The event brings together over 3,500 church and industry leaders and over 200 exhibitors from around the world to guide facilities and technology investments and opportunities for houses of worship.

This year's event will deliver on its theme, "WFX Gets You There," by offering attendees a newly updated Conference, dynamic keynote presentations, packed expo floor, networking opportunities, and tours of some of the most successful and innovative churches in the Charlotte area. Designed for decision-making teams from churches of all sizes, the goal is to deliver exceptional learning opportunities and showcase state-of-the-art products and services designed to help churches achieve their ministry goals.[3]

Here is an event about how to be a faithful steward of buildings and equipment used in glorifying God, and yet the language is permeated with the language of business and management: "technology investments and opportunities," "dynamic keynote speakers," "packed expo floor," "networking opportunities," "tours of some of the most successful and innovative churches," "designed for decision-making teams," "showcase state-of-the-art products and services," "achieve ministry goals."

This promotional, managerial language is used more and more in the church, but fewer and fewer Christians are noticing how the fundamental way we think about the church has shifted.

It's understandable why we are enamored with this approach: it gives the illusion of control and order. It allows us to manipulate people and institutions so that they perform on cue, so that we also can have "successful and innovative churches." Those are much easier churches to manage than Spirit-filled churches. We can look to the world of business and find thousands of case studies that will show us state-of-the-art techniques to help us solve any particular organizational hurdle that gets in the way of success.

Look to the Holy Spirit, on the other hand, and you might find him managing us and doing things that seem to undermine our ministry goals—like pulling us out of a densely populated area ripe with effective ministry opportunities into a desert where we see no opportunities for ministry whatsoever.

❧

Let me clarify that I'm not against megachurches any more than I'm against grand cathedral churches. No doubt the Holy Spirit has raised up many of these institutions. Worshiping with thousands of fellow believers encourages and inspires in extraordinary ways. And the variety of ministries a megachurch can offer is impressive.

That being said, and as many megachurch leaders themselves are quick to acknowledge, large churches today can create a subculture—and a way of thinking about church that even infects smaller congregations—that makes it difficult to listen to the Spirit. The wealthy, Jesus says, can only get into heaven through the eye of a needle; the same applies to churches wealthy in numbers and programs.

In an insightful Hartford Institute for Religion Research study, Scott Thumma explores the many dynamics that are required to create and sustain a megachurch.[4] One of those dynamics is that the megachurch easily becomes a religious business. One pastor interviewed said that as his church grew into megachurch proportions, he found himself "acting more like a mayor or governor than a pastor."

The sheer size of a megachurch demands an emphasis on efficiency, and that means an emphasis on bureaucracy, systems, and organization, with a corresponding decline on ministering to people as individuals. Of course, the megachurch staff will argue that all the systems are in place on behalf of people, but the emphasis on systems is no more or less the law of any bureaucracy. And we all know what it feels like when a bureaucrat tries to convince us that all the paperwork and the following of procedures is really for our best interest: we know we've entered a world where the institution has become preeminent.

150

A staff member of one megachurch defended this way of doing church work: "We are a church but we are also a business that happens to be operating by the name of a church. We are a ten-million-dollar-a-year church that has to operate like a business." He obviously felt conflicted about this, suspecting that somewhere along the way he had forgotten what a church was really about. He believed he had no choice but to view his church as a religious business, but at the same time, he admitted, "As the church has gotten so huge, it's harder to make decisions based on an understanding of the Holy Spirit's leading. . . . By the time [a spiritual decision] gets down to the implementation level, it's nothing but sort of a bureaucratic 'do this' or 'do that.' "

"Do this" and "Do that" is not merely the lifestyle of megachurches. It has become the preferred lifestyle of most North American Christians. As Thumma's megachurch study notes:

Megachurch members are at home in large scale institutions (Ostling 1991; Schaller 1992). They grew up in them and were nurtured by them. They were probably born in a giant hospital, educated in a consolidated high school and large public university, and entertained by rock concerts, cable television, and multiplex movie theaters. No doubt they shop in malls and food warehouses, and may commute thirty minutes or more to jobs in large corporations situated in office parks. These institutional realities and their practices have shaped both the character and the needs of these people.

This is one reason so many of us feel "at home" in a megachurch. We all have been shaped by the ethos of these large institutions, where efficiency and effectiveness are prime values. It is no surprise that those values make their way into our individual and daily lives. It's all part of an ambience we try to create, an ambience of control and order.

We regularly complain about our busy lives, but then we set up systems that ensure that we will live no other way. Our spiritual lives are integrated with the rest of our lives in a seemly pattern of efficiency. Morning prayer becomes a fixed routine that takes no more than ten minutes. We always look for the fastest way to drive from here to there, leaving here with just enough time to get there—and so we never really have time to pull over and help a stranded motorist because, well, we're running late. Foods become mere delivery systems of nutrients rather than gifts that help us bask in God's goodness—we spend more time looking at the nutrient chart on the label than thinking about the joy the food might bring us. We want relationships, except when the friend becomes needy, at which point we give them a lecture about codependency. Worship is very important to us, at least for sixty minutes, but then doesn't the pastor understand we have things to do?

And on it goes. It's really rather comical. We say we long for intimacy with God and others, and yet we structure our lives so that this becomes impossible. One might think we are avoiding intimacy, that maybe we really like our finely managed lives just the way they are. Well, I can speak for one person and acknowledge that this is true for me more often than I care to admit.

This makes for a life in which we get a lot done, in which we move up in the world, in which we get the most out of life. It is efficient and effective, managerial and businesslike. People who organize themselves in this way have high status in our culture, and many write books and lead seminars telling other people how to emulate them. There is a certain satisfaction in managing one's day and one's life like this, a satisfying feeling of accomplishment at meeting goals and objectives. Again, anyone who knows me knows that I am speaking autobiographically here.

No question that the Spirit can make use of such people, despite their deafness to his leading much of the time. But how much richer—even if less efficient—would our lives be if we, like Philip, were willing to be carried away by the Spirit once in a while.

❧

As we've noted, after leaving a stunningly fruitful urban ministry, Philip ended up in the middle of nowhere. As the Spirit would have it, he was more interested in Philip ministering to one exotic foreigner than to hundreds if not thousands of city folk. After Philip got to the desert, he ran across an Ethiopian court official and was instrumental in the official's conversion and baptism.

As that episode concluded, Luke notes, "And when they came up out of the water, the Spirit of the Lord carried Philip away, and the eunuch saw him no more, and went on his way rejoicing" (Acts 8:39).

The way Luke puts this has puzzled many a commentator. It sounds as if the Spirit physically lifted Philip up and carried him away, as an eagle might pick up and carry away its prey. Rationalists among us immediately balk and think this must be a euphemism for the Spirit's normal leading—getting a sense of direction and following it in faith. In fact, Luke isn't really interested in describing exactly what being carried away by the Spirit might look like. Luke is mainly trying to communicate that Philip was anything but in control here, that a sense of decency and order was not Philip's highest priority. Living under the dynamic, freeing leadership of the Spirit was.

In the end, of course, it's not an either-or. God gifts each of us with some measure of organizational intelligence, and he expects us, as rational creatures, to manage our lives in such a way that they bring glory to him. That means managing not just our emotions and our will but also the details of our day-to-day lives. We are stewards of something precious and extraordinary, and he longs to tell us at the end, as he scans our lives, "Well done, good and faithful servant" (Matt. 25:21).

But it's not hard to see how quickly stewardship of our time becomes a means to control and order our lives, rather than an opportunity to begin each day asking, "Spirit of God, to where will you carry me today?" Most likely it will be to the usual places, where we'll meet the usual assortment of people. Once in a while, he'll call us to forsake the golden opportunity in order to send us to the desert. Other times he'll magically transport us to a place or calling we would never have imagined possible. But even when he again carries us back to the same office and classroom, to the same people we meet every day, we will know this: that our lives are not our own, and that the Spirit has given us these people and this place to do God's work.

If that is not liberating, I don't know what is. Scary, to be sure. Requiring more faith than we seem to have on most days. But imagine how freeing it would be to release the death grip we have on our lives and just let the gracious and loving Spirit of Jesus carry us where he would each day.

17

FROM SHAME TO OBEDIENCE

Ananias lived far away from the action. Damascus was no mean city, but it lay nearly two hundred miles from Jerusalem, where the Spirit was doing marvelous things day after day. Eruption of ecstatic languages. Healings. Miracles. Dreams and visions. How Ananias became a Christian we do not know, but we can assume that some of the disciples who had been scattered by the first pogrom against Christians (see Acts 8:1–4) had brought the message of Jesus there. Enough Christians had sprung up in Damascus that Saul thought it worth a trip to root them out. But we hear nothing of the miraculous in Damascus as we have in Jerusalem.

Until Ananias has his divine visitation. Ananias doesn't doubt he is being addressed by the resurrected Jesus. He is not like Samuel who, when the Lord called him, was confused, thinking it was the voice of his mentor Eli (see 1 Sam. 3:1–10). Ananias knows who is speaking to him: "Here I am, Lord," he replies (Acts 9:10).

It's when the Lord gives him a specific instruction that things get complicated. "Rise and go to the street called Straight, and at the house of Judas look for a man of Tarsus named Saul, for behold, he is praying," says the Lord, "and he has seen in a vision a man named Ananias come in and lay his hands on him so that he might regain his sight" (Acts 9:11–12).

There is a lot here that Ananias takes for granted—that there is a man named Saul at the house of Judas on Straight Street, that Saul is blind, that Ananias will be able to heal him. In this respect, everything about the command makes sense to Ananias.

Most of us would balk at the social awkwardness of following through. "Hi, Saul. My name is Ananias, and the Lord told me to come here." You don't have to live in a skeptical age like ours to recognize that such a greeting would mark you as a religious fanatic.

Or maybe we'd run from the potential foolishness. Let's assume that a skeptical Saul invites the religious fanatic in and gives him permission to pray for his healing. At such a moment, doubts would assail most of us: *What exactly do I pray for? That doctors and nurses will be given wisdom to heal Saul? That Saul will be healed inwardly of his spiritual blindness? That Saul will actually be given his sight? But what if I pray and nothing happens?*

In such moments, many fears assault us and deprive us of our freedom to respond naturally, willingly to the divine command. But the only thing that concerns Ananias is the man he is told to meet: "Lord, I have heard from many about this man, how much evil he has done to your saints at Jerusalem. And here he has authority from the chief priests to bind all who call on your name" (Acts 9:13–14).

Saul's reputation has preceded him, and it has left a deep impression on Ananias. Saul was not someone a Christian would want to meet if he valued his freedom. Ananias knows the risks involved and wants to avoid them. It is a moment of spiritual chaos for Ananias.

The Lord, of course, presses Ananias, telling him that the point of this risk-fraught enterprise is the healing and calling of another, so that the gospel might go forth even more splendidly. To this "logic," Ananias relents. He does what he believes the Lord wants of him. And of course, the vision becomes a reality: Saul is healed and does indeed become a divine instrument for the preaching of the Good News across the known world.

This is one of many stories in the book of Acts, not to mention the whole Bible, in which someone is asked to release control of his life to obey a simple but risk-filled command of the Lord.

One Sunday morning I was in Stockholm, Sweden, visiting a church. The pastor was finishing a sermon on love in the Christian community. In the application, he emphasized how small groups can create and sustain a sense of community. That's when a thought popped into my head: *You should definitely start the home Bible study you've been thinking about for months.*

I wondered if this was a Spirit-inspired thought. Like Ananias and unlike Samuel, I suspected that this was a word from the Lord. In my own way, I inwardly said, "Here I am, Lord," and I resolved to start a Bible study when I returned to the States.

After the sermon, the pastor explained that during the next hymn, prayer ministers would stand at the front of the sanctuary to pray for anyone who came forward. And then as the hymn began, another thought popped into my head: *You should go up for prayer for the home Bible study you want to start.*

That's when the wrestling began.

At my home church, I have on occasion availed myself of a prayer minister during worship. Every Sunday, many in our parish do the same. So it would not have been out of character for me to do so in this Swedish congregation.

Neither was language a barrier. The service was in Swedish, yes, but it was translated through headphones in English. And every Swede I had met on this trip could converse in English. So I assumed that one of the prayer ministers would be able to communicate with me.

The problem was that no one in the congregation stepped forward. With six prayer ministers standing at the front, I figured that a slew of people would step up, but no such thing happened. I surmised that either no one felt moved to do so this morning, or this was a new custom the pastoral staff was trying to introduce to the congregation.

In any event, I now squirmed. On the one hand, the urging to go forward for prayer was just as strong as the urge to start a home Bible study, and I attributed both to the nudging of the Spirit. But the second nudge required a public commitment in a setting in which I was a stranger. Going forward alone would have drawn a great deal of attention to me.

So what? I debated. *I'll never see these people again. And maybe the sight of one person, a visitor no less, going forward will encourage others to do so.*

Then again, I thought, *But what will they think I'm seeking prayer for?* The minister had included in his invitation to prayer a call to commit one's life to Christ. I didn't want people thinking I hadn't already done that!

On this went through the hymn, until I finally defeated the Spirit, stubbornly staying rooted in my pew.

This, of course, is not an unusual situation for a Christian to find himself in, especially if he identifies with the broader evangelical movement. We have been invited to do such in one way or another in many such services. As British historian of evangelicalism David Bebbington has noted, *conversionism*—or what I call *decisionism*—is part and parcel of our Christian subculture.[1] The Christian life does not just evolve.

It also requires specific decisions and public commitments to deepen our faith and obedience.

We also believe that Christ is raised from the dead, alive and active in his Holy Spirit. He is Lord not only of the world but of our lives, a God who would guide us with his loving, even daily commands.

So we've had to learn how to negotiate such moments—knowing that not every thought that pops into our head is from the Spirit, *and knowing full well that some of them are!* We've all looked back in gratitude at moments when our response seems to have been prompted by the Spirit.

A woman is having a dinner party, and the name of someone she just met pops into her head. She takes it as a nudging of the Spirit, and so she invites the man. During the meal, this man gets into a deep conversation with another guest, and the topic turns to vocation. By the end of the evening, the man, who already is settled in a career, starts thinking about changing jobs. He eventually quits his job, applies for graduate school, and starts working in a whole new field. This is the sort of serendipity that many have been a part of.

Then again, we've all looked back in retrospect with regret at some decision, realizing it was not a response to the Spirit but to pressures of others or the ego. This is not something we talk about much, especially in the chattering classes—writers, speakers, professors, public intellectuals, and so forth. And as mature adults (some of us quite mature in years, anyway), we certainly don't like to admit that peer pressure can sway us as much as it does adolescents. But if our theology is correct—that Christ is alive in the Spirit, that we are in a personal relationship with a God who at times actively guides our lives—well, we all have to be wrestling with, and often repenting about, such matters.

I had just finished attending the Pentecostal World Conference in Sweden when I went to this church, so my spiritual antennae were especially alert. While I don't call myself a Pentecostal, I am sure Pentecostals would accept some of my spiritual experiences as evidence of "Spirit baptism" and thus welcome me into the fold. So there is certainly much in the movement that I resonate with. Personal negotiations with the Spirit would be one of them.

But when I asked theologians and pastors at the conference how Pentecostals discerned the leading of the Spirit—that is, how they determined when it was the Spirit and when it was not—they didn't have a lot to say. Pentecostals as a group pretty much rely on the subjective sense to determine this, they said.

This strikes me as woefully insufficient and subject to abuse—to which many of the Pentecostals I spoke with agreed. They granted that there were excesses and even abuses. But their answers seemed to suggest that you can hardly have a dynamic, Spirit-led movement among weak, sinful, and foolish human beings and expect it to be perfect.

One does have to acknowledge that for all the excesses and abuses, the movement is changing lives and the face of world Christianity. It does indeed seem to be a Spirit-led movement.

That got me to thinking about how God gets his work done in this world. I would like to think that he does so mainly through people professionally or spiritually qualified—people of discernment, wise in the ways of both the world and the Spirit. But this is precisely what he does not seem to do, or to do consistently. Whole continents are being transformed by Pentecostals, who are the first to say they identify wholeheartedly with Paul:

> For consider your calling, brothers: not many of you were wise according to worldly standards, not many were powerful, not many were of noble birth. But God chose what is foolish in the world to shame the wise; God chose what is weak in

the world to shame the strong; God chose what is low and despised in the world, even things that are not, to bring to nothing things that are, so that no human being might boast in the presence of God. (1 Cor. 1:26–29)

North American Christians, and evangelicals in particular, have long ago abandoned the idea that we are foolish, weak, low, and despised. We've been striving for some time to prove to our culture—and maybe to ourselves—that we are anything but those things. Pentecostals seem to revel in them.

In the end, I don't believe God honors foolishness—think of all those biblical verses extolling the virtue of wisdom. Furthermore, the arc of the Bible is to strengthen the weak and raise the lowly and despised. That being said, God seems most to honor the humble and contrite heart (see Ps. 51:17)—whether foolish or wise, whether weak or strong.

Here's how I've seen it work time and again. Joe Christian thinks Jesus is telling him to do X, Y, and Z. It seems to me that Joe is confused and that a lot of X, Y, and Z is wrapped up in delusions of spiritual grandeur—lots of inflated talk about "transforming the culture" or "blessing the nations" or "healing" or "prosperity." And yet God seems to bless the life and ministry of Joe, despite obvious theological problems and seeming improprieties. God has this uncanny knack of using people I consider unqualified in one way or another to touch many lives with his love and justice.

I've concluded that God often does not care if we guess his will correctly. If this was a high priority, he'd be a lot clearer about making his will plain! A higher priority for him seems to be this: humble and contrite hearts that are willing to risk, to step into the unknown just because it *might be* God's will. He honors the heart as much as the execution.

When my daughter Katie was a girl, she learned calligraphy. At the time, I showed her a quote I said I wanted to have in calligraphy someday. She soon presented me with the quote, framed and in her newly learned art.

161

It was not good, I have to say—a judgment she doesn't disagree with today as an adult. Lines swayed helplessly, and some letters looked like they were going to fall over. It was clearly an amateur effort. But she was proud of it.

And so was I. I happily displayed it on my office wall for years. It was not what I had envisioned, but it was something that despite its imperfections—and partly because of them—I cherished.

Okay, it's a cheesy illustration, the kind that sophisticated people like me are not supposed to traffic in. But, to paraphrase Paul, God often uses the cheesy to confound the sophisticated. He regularly honors those who are confused about his leading as if they have nailed it.

Did the Spirit prompt me to go forward to receive prayer? If you press me, I might agree that I have no way of knowing for sure, but I suspect he did. I also increasingly suspect that God wants me to be more willing to do a seemingly foolish thing because I merely suspect it *might be* something he's calling me to do. It's not that I should ignore wisdom that comes through the community of faith or Scripture. But what's as important, it seems, is a willingness to put wisdom, wealth, strength, and honor on the line if I believe that maybe, just maybe, the Spirit is leading me to do so.

Whenever we wrestle with the Spirit like this, we wrestle with that original sin: the desire to order our lives, the yearning to control the shape of our existence. In many instances, that takes the form of wanting to control our reputation. Most reading this book do so in cultures in which the Sauls of this world have lost their power. In most places in the world, no one is running around breathing threats against Christians. But we know that if we do what the Lord asks of us, we may look foolish. And this, for us, feels as threatening as a Saul seeking our lives.

The paradox is that the fear of shame is already a prison. That fear binds us as strong as any chain, preventing us from doing those things that the Lord calls us to do. And it is often at the very point of our fear that the Spirit prods us, presses us, pushes us. Not out of meanness, of course, but only to create freedom—for ourselves as we obey and for the other to whom we are called to minister.

Like the person Ananias was called to minister to: Saul, the scales on whose eyes fell so that he could see again. It was that possibility—that a Saul could be turned into one who could proclaim "For freedom Christ has set us free" (Gal. 5:1)—that prompted Ananias to release this grip on not only his reputation but his life and to enter into a deeper level of liberty in Christ.

18

FROM POWER TO PROMISE

If I didn't know better, I would have concluded that the story of Simon the Magician was created and inserted into Acts 8 by an American writer. Simon is just so American, which is why I can't get as upset with him as was Peter. You can't help but admire the man's practicality and initiative.

Simon was a man who knew about power. That's what "magic" is—the manipulation of nature or divinities to accomplish one's ends. Simon was not just good at his craft but "great," according to popular opinion. The entire region—from the socially lowest to urbane highest—was enamored with him. He was Peyton Manning, Warren Buffett, and Bono rolled into one. He was *the* rock star of Samaria, the superhero of the region.

And then he became a Christian. He listened to the preaching of Philip and recognized the existence of someone more powerful than himself, and he bent the knee to Jesus. He tagged along with his new mentor, Peter, and was fascinated by the repeated "signs and great miracles" that were performed (v. 13). The amazing Simon was himself amazed.

But he had seen nothing yet. When Peter and John laid hands on the new Samaritan believers, they received an extraordinary filling of the Spirit—evidenced likely by speaking in tongues or other displays of ecstasy.[1] Simon was bowled over.

"Give me this power also," he stammered, "so that anyone on whom I lay my hands may receive the Holy Spirit" (v. 19).

You could probably hear the proverbial pin drop as the apostles gaped in wide-eyed shock at Simon and then one another.

When Peter collected himself, he let Simon have it: "To hell with your money!" That's the more literal rendering of the formal translation, "May your silver perish with you" (v. 20). Peter read the heart of Simon and saw that it was "not right before God" (v. 21), that Simon was "in the gall of bitterness and in the bond of iniquity" (v. 23).

But Simon was just a man ahead of his time. He was acting like a pragmatic American. And because of this we should have some empathy toward him.

Simon did two things we do as a matter of course today.

First, he was simply trying to baptize the talents and resources of his former life. He wanted to make use of those gifts in the service of his new master, Jesus. Converted artists want to use their art for Christ, just as converted carpenters want to use their woodworking skills. Simon was a man comfortable with power. He knew how to manipulate it. He knew how to impress people with it. So he was looking for a way to employ it for Jesus.

He saw the extraordinary power of the Holy Spirit falling on these believers, and he recognized its potential. This is the sort of thing that would have made his previous magical works pale by comparison. This power wasn't merely about wonderful displays, like fireworks, but a power that moved mountains, like dynamite. This power actually changed people and had the power to change society. Simon knew power, and he savored the possibilities at hand.

Second, Simon assumed that this sort of power could be as easily manipulated as any sort of power. And that manipulation begins, as it always does, with wealth. If you have enough money, the thinking goes, you can do anything.

Simon can be forgiven, for he was a new Christian. He reminds me of a young man I once counseled. He had just become a Christian, and he had also just been brought up to a Triple-A baseball team. Living in a strange city, he was looking for support, so he phoned the church I was working at and asked me to come and pray with him weekly. In the course of our conversations, it became clear that he believed that the power of the Holy Spirit was helping him hit more home runs. Not in the sense that he had more confidence at the plate or more calm when facing tough pitchers. No, he thought that when the Bible talked about the Holy Spirit giving people power, it meant physical power. When I gently explained to him the nature of spiritual power, he was a little disappointed. So I can understand Simon's confusion, coming out of a background of paganism as he did.

This doesn't mean that he didn't deserve a dressing down. Sometimes that's the only way we'll be shocked out of bad beliefs. For someone to tell us pointedly that we're being foolish can be an act of love. Peter's strong talk was a gift of the Spirit, the Spirit who introduces confusion and chaos into our lives to bring us to new places of freedom. Simon needed his assumptions about power to be rattled.

So do we. We know better than to think we can buy the Holy Spirit with money. But we are as fascinated with spiritual power as Simon was, and we nonetheless think that it is up for barter. If we play our cards right, God will surely give us the power we want—the power to change ourselves and our world.

There is in the soul of American Christianity a feverish anxiety. If, as a result of our faith in Christ, we do not experience moral uplift, we jump-start a new spiritual formation regimen. If the church is not making a difference in the world, we shame ourselves to become more socially relevant and evangelistically effective. In short, we look for power—power to transform our ugly lives into something beautiful, power to transform a sick society into something healthy.

This anxiety is concentrated at the personal level. It is a deep longing for personal transformation in those areas that most frustrate and discourage us. I once wrote a column in which I argued that the change the Bible talks about is not complete but only partial in this life. The response from many readers suggested that they not only disagreed but were banking their lives on change. Here are three comments (all the caps are in the original):

> Christ's death not only freed us from the penalty of sin, but from the power of sin in this life. I am a witness. CHANGE HAPPENS.

> Grace causes us to have changed lives. Or maybe u haven't read Ephesians 2 really well.

> My concern must be to live the life GOD called me to live AT THIS MOMENT! I CAN CHANGE!!

In other words, the Christian faith is meaningful because it promises change. We are fed up with the tragedy of our lives—the failures and flaws, the coarse habits and endless addictions, the inability to do the good that we long to do consistently and sincerely. In pragmatic, practical America, we look for a faith that can solve this problem. What good is a religion if it doesn't give us the power to change?

But of course, the power that most interests us and the power the Christian faith promises are two different things. We need a good talking-to, as well.

Contrary to our aspirations and assumptions, the Christian faith is not a bulleted list of things we do that enable us to live the good life, let alone the best life now. Nor does it present us with an agenda, as some would have it, for making the world a better place. Our faith is not primarily a program or a power for change. The core of the faith is good *news*. It is a revelation of the deeper realities that plague us (of which our anxiety about change is just a symptom) and the unveiling of an unshakable hope.

As Michael Horton puts it in his *Christless Christianity*, "You don't need Jesus to have better families, finances, health, or even morality."[2] Lots of religions, therapies, and self-help regimens enable people to break addictions, control tempers, repair relationships, and even practice forgiveness. Many social reform groups serve the neighbor. At this level of ethics, God appears to work through many means besides the church.

The Good News drills down deeper than this. As Horton says, "Coming to the cross means repentance—not adding Jesus as a supporting character for an otherwise decent script, but throwing away the script in order to be written into God's drama. It is death and resurrection, not coaching and makeovers."[3] The deeper reality is that our alienation is not from our better self—the thing we're most interested in improving—but from the Creator of that self. This alienation is fixed and certain. It demands not a makeover but a start over, a start over so complete that it begins with death.

But how can we speak of starting over with death, when death speaks of the end of all possibilities, the end of power, the end of the ability to control our lives? It doesn't make sense, so we try to scratch and claw our way to a better life now, so anxious are we to find and use any power that can change us.

But the Good News is not that God so loved the world that he gave his Son so we could become better people. It is: "God so loved the world, that he gave his only Son, that whoever believes in him should not perish but have eternal life" (John 3:16).

We are not called to imitate the Lord Jesus Christ so that we shall be transformed. No, we imitate Christ because first we are promised, "If you confess with your mouth that Jesus is Lord and believe in your heart that God raised him from the dead, you will be saved" (Rom. 10:9). The Good News does not hinge on words like *do* or *change* but on the powerless, irrelevant, and frightening words like *belief* and *faith*.

Faith is frightening because it speaks of the death of the self—the death of our power to control and order our moral lives. Faith seems weak and useless because it seems to undermine any role we might play in this salvation drama.

Here I must repeat what I said in an earlier chapter, so crucial is it for our understanding: Faith is not an *attitude* or mere intellectual *assent* or *a repentant and contrite heart*. It is not something we work up to impress God. Faith is the sudden realization that God has done something remarkable in the crucifixion and resurrection of Jesus Christ—we've been crucified and raised with Christ. No ifs, ands, or buts.

It is the no-strings character of grace that demolishes our usual view of change and of power. The free gift must remain absolutely free if we are going to be transformed in the way God calls us to be transformed—if (as Jesus says) we really are to surpass the legalistic righteousness of the Pharisees, if (as Paul exhorts) we really are to exhibit the fruit of the Spirit, the first of which is love.

If faith is any way a deal—we believe and then God gives us the power to change—then we will never be free from the inordinate desire for control and order, and in this case, the addiction to power to change our lives. We would merely be using God like an alcoholic uses liquor. God is a means to an end—our transformation! Such a relationship with God is characterized by many things—manipulation, coercion, fear, resentment, striving—but it cannot be characterized by love.

Furthermore, the yearning for the power to change—and thus for that perennial temptation for order and control—is like an alcoholic yearning for a drink to get ahold of himself. At first it feels like it's working. But as the alcoholic drinks more and more, alcohol only makes things worse. It's only when he releases his desire for control—admits his life is out of control and submits himself to a higher power—that he paradoxically is given the type of power the Bible is interested in.

Only unconditional grace can transform a hardened heart into a grateful heart. Only a free gift can demolish any notion of the quid pro quo. Only an utterly merciful act of love can fashion a new creation capable of love. As theologian Karl Barth puts it, "As the beloved of God, we have no alternative but to love him in return."[4]

We pragmatic American Christians are always tempted to turn the Christian life into a program for moral improvement, when really Christ is about freeing us from anxiety about moral improvement! Certainly there will be moral improvement, addictions healed, virtues strengthened—Christ is indeed transforming us. But these are not the result of our manipulating some power or program for self-improvement or social change. These come as a by-product of having relinquished the whole idea that we are in control of that change. It is God working in us, to do as he wills.

The paradox is that we really have to abandon all desire for change—that is, all desire to control and order a new life for ourselves or for our society—before any significant change can occur. God will determine when and how and by what means change will happen. And a careful reading of history suggests he is much more patient about change than we are. As we look within ourselves and around us at fellow believers, we see a lot that still hasn't changed.

This is not a cause for discouragement, though, nor the time for another pep talk to be better. Instead, declared Martin Luther, "Be a sinner and sin boldly, but believe and rejoice in Christ even more boldly. For he is victorious over sin, death, and the world. As long as we are here, we have to sin. This life is not the dwelling place of righteousness but, as Peter says, we look for a new heavens and a new earth in which righteousness dwells. . . . Pray boldly—you too are a mighty sinner."[5]

In fact, Paul himself, even at the end of his life, after decades of living for Christ, thinks of himself only as the foremost of sinners (see 1 Tim. 1:15). This does not sound like a man who has gained moral mastery over his life. And yet Paul seems unfazed. He remains confident of his transformation in Christ. This greatest of sinners can say boldly, "If anyone is in Christ, he is a new creation; old things have passed away; behold, all things have become new!" (2 Cor. 5:17 NKJV). All his letters assume that, in wonder and gratitude, we will "grow up in every way into him who is the head, into Christ" (Eph. 4:15), and he assumes that the Christian will show signs of that growth!

Paul remains unfazed because, though he is still "of the flesh, sold under sin" (Rom. 7:14), he lives by the *promise* that *someday* we will be set free and "obtain the freedom of the glory of the children of God" (Rom. 8:21). While exhorting us always to let our gratitude for God's forgiveness overflow into works of love, he never imagines that our moral progress will be worth writing home about—our bodies are dead because of sin (see Rom. 8:10)! Admiring our moral improvement is like looking at our loved one stretched out in a casket and commenting on how good he looks in that suit—for all the good it's going to do him!

Instead Paul sets his eyes on a *promised* transformation. "Behold! I tell you a mystery. . . . We shall all be changed," he tells those immoral Corinthians. "For the trumpet will sound, and the dead will be raised imperishable, and we shall be changed" (1 Cor. 15:51–52). Though he is speaking specifically about our resurrected bodies, his entire theology points not to the present but to the future. It's a theology not of present signs and wonders but of promised glory.

It's like this: We've won the lottery of life, and we hold the winning ticket. It's only a matter of getting to the lottery office to cash it in. We are full with child, and it's only a matter of time before a breathing baby comes forth. A down payment has been made on our ideal home, and it's only a matter of time before we can move in. We live in hope!

In the meantime, we're living in the meantime. And the meantime can be a terrible time, full of selfishness and vanity, murder and greed, and subject to decay—as our bodies and souls know all too well.

As Martin Luther put it, the Christian is "at one and the same time a sinner and a righteous person. He is a sinner in fact, but a righteous person by the sure reckoning and promise of God that he will continue to deliver him from sin until he has completely cured him. And so he is totally healthy in hope, but a sinner in fact. He has the beginning of righteousness, and so always continues more and more to seek it, while realizing that he is always unrighteous."[6]

If we live in this hope, we will be free of the temptation to barter with God for the power of the Holy Spirit. We will be free from the anxiety about our moral improvement, free from our fantasies of changing the world, free to live lives of uncoerced love.

It is not an easy thing to discover and live in such freedom. It's certainly not something we can will by some inner power. No, Simon got it right when he asked Peter, "Pray for me to the Lord" (Acts 8:24). But not to worry. This is the type of prayer the Lord loves to answer.

19

FROM UTOPIA TO CHURCH

One can get easily fooled about the early church by cherry-picking passages from Acts, like this one:

> And they devoted themselves to the apostles' teaching and the fellowship, to the breaking of bread and the prayers. And awe came upon every soul, and many wonders and signs were being done through the apostles. And all who believed were together and had all things in common. And they were selling their possessions and belongings and distributing the proceeds to all, as any had need. And day by day, attending the temple together and breaking bread in their homes, they received their food with glad and generous hearts, praising God and having favor with all the people. And the Lord added to their number day by day those who were being saved. (2:42–47)

Such passages dazzle us. What faith! What community! What Christlike behavior! Such passages elicit a fair number of sermons extolling the glories of the early church, accompanied by chastisements for us to do better.

But spending a little more time in Acts is like spending a little more time in a church you've just joined. You soon get over the honeymoon.

The first thing we discover is hypocrites. While a number of early believers sold their property and gave all the proceeds to the church, one couple, Ananias and Sapphira, only looked like they were doing that. Instead, they were keeping a little on the side for themselves (see 5:1–11).

The problem was not that they were hoarding. What concerned Peter was their lying. And just after this incident, Luke notes, "None of the rest dared join them, but the people held them in high esteem," followed by the seemingly contradictory, "And more than ever believers were added to the Lord" (5:13–14). I take "them" in the first clause to refer to those who were selling their possessions. More and more people were in fact joining the church, but not everyone was required to "join them"—that is, join those few who were selling all their possessions.

No, the problem was hypocrisy. Ananias and Sapphira were pretending to be more generous than they actually were.

Besides hypocrisy, we see signs of favoritism. We've already noted this when looking at the story of deacon Stephen. The fledgling church had already created a food distribution program for widows, who in that day were utterly dependent on the welfare of family and friends. Among the new believers were both Hellenists, who came out of a Greco-Roman subculture, and Hebrews, who were Jews in faith and culture. Since at this early stage most Christians were Hebrews, they had a natural affinity with the Hebrew widows. It appears that when they were running short of time or goods, Hebrew widows got served first (see 6:1).

We also see something worse: outright prejudice. While they were not yet considered full-fledged members of the church, at least Hellenist Jews were welcomed. But run-of-the-mill

Gentiles—that is, those lacking the distinctive mark of God's people, circumcision—were another thing. The early church had the hardest time accepting the simple command of Jesus to be "witnesses . . . to the end of the earth" (1:8). A mission to Gentiles remained unthinkable until the Holy Spirit forced the issue.

Paul had to be thrown to the ground, blinded, and then healed before he recognized his new mission: to carry the name of Christ "before the Gentiles" (9:15).

Then Peter had an extraordinary dream, combined with a moving encounter with the Gentile Cornelius, followed by a miraculous outpouring of the Spirit on a whole group of the uncircumcised before his ethnocentrism was shaken (see 10:1–43).

Finally, despite the stature of Peter and the rising stature of Paul, the rest of the church wasn't buying the new development: "But some men . . . were teaching the brothers, 'Unless you are circumcised according to the custom of Moses, you cannot be saved' " (15:1). This did not sit well with Paul and his missionary partner, for Luke notes, "Paul and Barnabas had no small dissension and debate with them" (15:2).

That little phrase "no small dissension" reveals a lot. This issue caused so much dissension in Antioch that the church there sought intervention by the mother church. So a delegation presented the issue before the leaders in Jerusalem, and the issue generated "much debate" (15:7). With the very identity of the new movement at stake, the debate was probably anything but charitable. It may be true that theology played a leading role in the debate, but given human nature, it's not hard to imagine that the desire for theological clarity was blended with simple prejudice.

So amidst the devotion, signs and wonders, and extraordinary sharing of goods, we see hypocrisy, favoritism, prejudice, and division. When the faith spreads to other Mediterranean cities, we see more of the same—and worse. In Galatia we see legalism; in Corinth, jealousy and incest; in Rome, judgmentalism; and so on. This is not the church of our dreams or a church composed of people with orderly, moral lives.

❧

We North American Christians come by our church idealism honestly. Europeans arrived in the American wilderness looking for Eden, and we've been looking for it ever since. John Winthrop, one of the founding Puritans, framed it in terms of community. In his famous "City on a Hill" speech, he described the "city" he and his fellow voyagers were hoping to establish:

> We must entertain each other in brotherly affection; we must be willing to abridge ourselves of our superfluities, for the supply of others' necessities. We must uphold a familiar commerce together in all meekness, gentleness, patience, and liberality. We must delight in each other; make others' conditions our own; rejoice together, mourn together, labor and suffer together, always having before our eyes our commission and community in the work, as members of the same body.[1]

This lovely vision became clouded within a generation, and Puritan preachers soon lamented the "great and visible decay of the power of Godliness amongst many."[2] The lament has been repeated by many an American preacher and writer since. We mock the angry revivalist for his self-righteous condemnation of backslidden believers, but beneath the jeremiad, huddled in the corner of his breast, is a weeping child, wounded and weary with the church, that community in which he had put so much hope and had only found disappointment.

While many wax eloquent about disappointment with God, just as many these days lament their disappointment with the church. At least one major book a year lately rehearses the lament. One year there was *unChristian: What a New Generation Really Thinks about Christianity . . . and Why It Matters* by David Kinnaman and Gabe Lyons.[3] The following year, *Washington Post* writer Julia Duin gave us *Quitting Church: Why the Faithful Are Fleeing and What to Do About It.*[4] More recent is Larry Crabb's *Real Church: Does It Exist? Can I Find It?*[5] Every year brings a fresh batch.

Such books often highlight studies that show that when it comes to rates of divorce, premarital sex, political bias, giving, or any number of moral or social issues, "evangelicals" or the "born again" or "conservative Christians" (depending on the survey) fare no better than the rest of America, and sometimes worse.

These facts are usually followed by the dismayed author asking, sometimes plaintively, sometimes prophetically, "Why does the church merely mirror the culture?" On the heels of righteous indignation come prescriptions and a pep talk. If the church would do X—anything from spiritual disciplines to church discipline to using more hip music—then the church would once again stand out as a city on a hill.

These studies convince because of personal experience. We enter door after church door, hoping to find a community where we can, in Winthrop's apt phrase, "delight in each other." What we bump into time and again is just a building full of people. Some delight in each other, all right, but to the point of excluding us. In other places, Winthrop's words about "meekness, gentleness, patience, and liberality" are but antonyms of what we experience. There is "labor and suffering," though not "together" but instead *against* one another. The church, we discover, is nothing but a house of sinners, a great and visible display of the "decay of the power of Godliness."

And so we empathize with many who leave the church and wander into the wilderness of faith alone. Both they and we long for a church, in the words of Crabb, that stands out "as an alternative community that offers what everyone was created to enjoy."[6] Or, as his title suggests, a "real" church.

I wonder, though, if in our search for a "real" church, we fail to see the actual church the Holy Spirit has created and with whom the Holy Spirit abides.

The yearning to be a part of a more holy church is partly a yearning for a perfect Eden, a memory of community we just can't shake. But this righteous longing is often mixed with an unrighteous one: a desire for order and control.

Like the desire to control the church's reputation. Many assume it is our job to make the church stand out from the culture, so that all the world will see what wonderful people we are and what a wonderful Savior we have. But God often makes himself known not through an impressive display of holiness but in spite of its lack. Often God makes his true nature known by hiding in the church, with all its sins and flaws, thus covering himself with the cloak of moral mediocrity.

As Isaiah put it, "Truly, you are a God who hides himself" (Isa. 45:15). He is the God who may have revealed himself in his law, but did so only through dark clouds and thick smoke (see Exod. 19:16–18). He may have come to us in Jesus, but he did so disguised, in the form of a servant, taking on flesh and blood. When God comes to us, well, you just can't pick him out of a crowd. Even after the resurrection—what more obvious proof do you want?—some still doubted (see Matt. 28:17).

If the church is the body of Christ in the world today, why would we think the world would be able to pick us out of a crowd of other well-meaning organizations?

The gospel is a treasure *hidden* in the field. It is the message given in perplexing parables so that, as Jesus said, "they may indeed see but not perceive, and may indeed hear but not understand" (Mark 4:12). This message will forever stupefy the educated, who look to it for cogent insights, and the pragmatic, who look to it to make a difference in the world: "For Jews demand signs and Greeks seek wisdom, but we preach Christ crucified, a stumbling block to Jews and folly to Gentiles" (1 Cor. 1:22–23).

Jesus said that weeds would grow up right along with the wheat, so that the church would look just like every other farm field. He also said there would be people who would look really devout—people who would pray, "Lord, Lord!" and who would prophesy and cast out demons and do mighty works—and yet who would not have a stitch of faith. Indeed, many will say "I'm an evangelical" or "I'm born again," and they will not know Jesus.

For his own unfathomable reasons, God chooses to disguise himself when he comes to this planet, and there have been few disguises better than the church.

This reality frustrates us, and so we often try to bring some order to the chaos that is the church. We browbeat one another: "The reason the world rejects Christian faith is the failure of the church to live Jesus's message." While we need to admonish one another to faithful obedience, often such admonitions are driven by our embarrassment with the church and our desire to protect God's reputation.

To be sure, God transforms his people. A church not witnessing some level of personal transformation in its members might want to do some serious soul-searching. But Jesus also told us to expect to find a lot of weeds in the church.

And he told us not to be anxious about getting rid of them—the very thing we're most tempted to do. We want to start pulling at the weeds, or at least spray some Roundup. I suspect Jesus knew that if we started controlling weeds, we'd end up killing ourselves.

That brings up the other area we have to relinquish control of. If the first is our desire to protect the church's reputation, the second is to protect our own. To be a member of the church the Holy Spirit has created and currently blesses—a weak, confused body of sinners—means to realize that I am a weed, no better nor worse than the rest of the bunch.

This is the path to freedom: releasing the idea that I have to be some paragon of virtue to be a real member of the real church. No, while we were sinners, Christ died for us and called us into his fellowship. I don't have to pretend that I have it together, that my life is an example of decency and order when, in fact, it is anything but that.

This is the church—with people like me in it—that Jesus is crazy in love with. This is the church he gave himself for. This church—even the church of the Inquisition and the Crusades and the Salem witch trials—is the church he puts his name on. He's like a father who has not been pleased of late with the athletic efforts of his son's miserable high school team, but who nonetheless proudly dons the school sweatshirt as he goes off to attend another game.

I sometimes wonder if God calls us into the church because it represents not the people of God at their best but us at our worst. I wonder if he calls us to become embedded in this wretched institution precisely because it is wretched. And calls us to be a part of it *not* to reform it or save it or control it in any way, but to simply love it.

Love is a call to abandon any notion that we're going to change others, manipulate their moral lives, or control their destiny. Love, in fact, will change them, but not in ways we can predict or program. To love with expectations is, in the end, an oppressive, driven thing, and people know it when they receive it. To love as God loves us—in freedom and with no strings attached—is a way to grant others a liberating gift. And as we've noted time and again, it's this uncoerced love that paradoxically "coerces" us to love and be transformed. Or as John put it, "we love because he first loved us" (1 John 4:19).

EPILOGUE

The reader with any moral sensibilities should be pretty nervous by now. As nervous as were the first recipients of Paul's letter to Rome.

In that magnificent treatise, Paul had to stop his argument five times in the first seven chapters to address one concern of the readers. He did this, no doubt, instinctively. Having presented in sermons the fabulous news of God's free grace on many occasions, he was well aware of the points at which listeners found the liberating gospel too good to be true. In Romans, this happens in these places:

Why not do evil that good may come? (3:8)

Do we then overthrow the law by this faith? (3:31)

Are we to continue in sin that grace may abound? (6:1)

Are we to sin because we are not under law but under grace? (6:15)

What then shall we say? That the law is sin? (7:7)

Morally sensible people get nervous when you start talking about grace as it's talked about in the Bible. In fact, we're not talking about grace if people aren't getting a little nervous, wondering if the religious house of cards we've created with morality or ritual or spirituality will collapse all around us. *Won't all this talk of grace and liberty just lead to anarchy?*

It's just at that point that we're starting to grasp the unbelievable nature of God's liberating love. This unsettling is but another movement of the Spirit, who is introducing the final touch into our overly controlled and ordered spiritual lives.

Paul drives home the point in his first letter to Corinth when he writes, " 'All things are lawful,' but not all things are helpful. 'All things are lawful,' but not all things build up" (1 Cor. 10:23). I believe he really means it when he says, "All things are lawful." That is, there really is no condemnation in Jesus Christ: "For the law of the Spirit of life has set you free in Christ Jesus from the law of sin and death" (Rom. 8:2).

This means we are free from religion, from mere morality, from ritual, from duties, from guilt, from shame—and from our fear of all these things. We really don't *have to* do anything. Grace is not a quid pro quo. It's not a deal. It's utterly free, leaving us utterly free. "For freedom Christ has set us free," writes Paul, "stand firm therefore, and do not submit again to a yoke of slavery" (Gal. 5:1).

As we've seen, two thousand years later, this Good News seems just too good to be true. I've just popped into eight places in the book of Acts that jumped out at me when I compared the spiritual freedom evident there with the spiritual handcuffs we so often find ourselves in today. The examples could be multiplied not only from Acts but from other books of the New Testament as well.

But of course, anyone who has grasped gospel freedom will instinctively agree with Paul: "For you were called to freedom, brothers. Only do not use your freedom as an opportunity for the flesh, but through love serve one another" (Gal. 5:13). Anyone who recognizes the extraordinary thing

God has done for us in Christ, who has been touched by the gracious liberty of the Spirit, cannot imagine doing anything else. Once you've encountered uncoerced love, you want nothing more than to respond in kind, to God and to neighbor.

In the end, the main problem with religion is not merely that it forfeits our liberty or that it feeds our desire for control. It mostly feeds our addiction to the self. It gives us a metaphysical rationale to spend our lives mired in the parochial and the trivial. Jesus did not come for the righteous but for sinners; not for those who are well but for the sick; not for the religious but for those who are suffering poverty, injustice, and spiritual alienation. He came in uncoerced love that we might be transformed to love the world as he does.

Naturally, we're still caught in and by our addiction much of the time. The instincts that the liberating Spirit would instill in us are still in formation. At times, when hyperbole gets the best of me, I talk as if this transformation is nearly automatic and simple. It is neither. It is both gift and struggle, joy and anguish. In one sentence Paul can talk about our transformation as if it were a done deal, and then in the next he exhorts his readers to "press on," "strain forward," and "stand firm" (Phil. 3:12–13; 4:1).

Nor is it easy to discern the dynamic leading of the liberating Spirit from "the desires of the flesh" (Gal. 5:16). Very often these look and feel the same. But of course, God knows we are weak and foolish. And so the law, from which we really are free, becomes not a demand but a guide, not an enemy but a friend. When we are confused about what it means to live in freedom, we can look to the law of God, interpreted by the law of love in the community of love, past and present.

This does not solve all the tensions inherent in the Spirit-led life, some of which, like the poor, will always be with us. But it does give us a foundation to live in confidence.

Yes, we mustn't be afraid. The liberty of the Spirit is a dangerous liberty, to be sure. It will be misunderstood and abused, if church history is any guide. Human nature being what it is, you cannot have a dynamic relationship with the liberating Spirit without there being questions, confusions, excesses, and mistakes—chaos. But if by God's grace, the man and the woman grew from the eating of the forbidden fruit, so will we grow when we discover that we've let our liberty get the better of us. All things—including our botched attempts to live in the Spirit—work together for the good.

Our maturity in Christ comes not from playing it safe. You do not learn to steal second in baseball by hugging first base. You never learn to swim unless you venture away from the side of the pool. The point of this book, and I believe the point of the Bible, is to help all of us to live more boldly and more openly—with one another and in the Spirit. We can indeed live as if Christ has set us free from anything that would bind us—disease or despair, injustice or legalism, social justice or moral reform, religion or ritual—and show a watching world (and a watching church) that grace is first and foremost a life of uncoerced love, in service to the world for whom Christ died.

A COMPANION GUIDE

This companion guide is designed to help groups reflect on the themes in *Chaos and Grace*. It is sparse enough to be easily supplemented with readings, songs, instruction, or other activities, depending on the energy and creativity of those planning the gatherings.

The questions are designed to elicit conversation. They may need to be rearranged or reworded to work best for your group. The questions are not designed to lead the group to some designated conclusion. If the chapter under discussion is persuasive, the conversation will end up affirming the theme. If not, some other perspectives and insights will emerge. When it comes to book discussions, people often learn more when they disagree with an author.

Questions mix the theological and the personal. The leader will want to mix and match depending on the personality of the group.

In any case, an atmosphere of freedom should characterize the discussion. The point of the book—and therefore this companion guide—is to become aware of the liberating work of the Holy Spirit.

Chapter 1: The Religious Captivity of the Church

Why God would entrust the church with these risky means of grace—worship, the Bible, preaching, and so forth—calling us to speak of the dangerous mercy of his firebrand Son through the mysterious power of the Spirit, I have no idea. But this God seems addicted to risk rather than religion, to freedom rather than control, to love rather than law.

from page 33

1. Read Acts 6:1–7:60.
2. What is most surprising to you about Stephen's speech?
3. What do you think made the listeners so angry?
4. Is "religion" a necessary evil or a positive good?
5. Are Christians too religious or not religious enough?
6. Can you imagine a form of Christianity in which religion did not play a significant role?
7. Where in your church's life do you see signs of healthy religion? Of religion that threatens to become toxic?
8. Where in your church do you think the power of the Spirit needs to be unleashed?

Chapter 2: The Eucatastrophe

From a state of perfect peace and harmony, [the planet] had been transformed in a few short days into a lush, rich, infinitely varied cacophony of color and sound and life. This is the sort of thing that happens when the Spirit of God tinkers.

from page 37

1. Read Genesis 1.
2. What most strikes you about the creation account?
3. What questions does it raise in your mind?
4. What is most persuasive in the author's interpretation?
5. What is least persuasive?

6. In your view, of the various types of chaos we encounter in life, which do you think are by God's design, and which are the result of the fall?

Chapter 3: Another Eucatastrophe

The fate of the man and the woman is to live in the knowledge of both glory *and* curse, good *and* evil, life *and* death—side by side, even woven together, forever. Well, not quite forever. For God in his goodness will not countenance a full-scale disaster.

from page 46

1. Read Genesis 2 and 3.
2. What strikes you most about the story of the fall?
3. What questions does it raise in your mind?
4. What is most persuasive in the author's interpretation?
5. What is least persuasive?
6. In your view, has anything good come of the fall?
7. What is the most important takeaway for you?

Chapter 4: Control Addiction

Story after story in Genesis repeats the same story, relives the same curse, in which people succumb over and over to the same addiction.

from page 49

1. Read Genesis 11.
2. What strikes you most about the story?
3. What questions does it raise in your mind?
4. What is most persuasive in the author's interpretation?
5. What is least persuasive?
6. Is the phrase "addiction to control" a helpful way to understand the consequences of the fall?

7. Do you think the main problem with human beings is that we are too controlling or not in control enough?
8. What about in your own life—which is the greater temptation?

Chapter 5: The Ordeal and the Promise

[Abraham's] has been a pilgrimage dark and impenetrable—in which hope was mixed with despair, free trust mingled with a desire to control, and the threat of death with resurrection.

from page 61

1. Read Genesis 12–17; 21:1–7; and 22:1–19.
2. What strikes you most about the story?
3. What questions does it raise in your mind?
4. What is most persuasive in the author's interpretation?
5. What is least persuasive?
6. Read Hebrews 11:8–19. Is it possible to admire Abraham's faith if the author's interpretation is correct? Why or why not?
7. What part of your own life do you see in Abraham?

Chapter 6: Early Signs of Liberation

History is the monotonous tale of the rise and fall of great civilizations—of growing power, control, and oppression of one group, followed by that of another. The language of liberation is often used to justify the overthrow of one regime, but it is not long before oppression characterizes the rule of the "liberators."

from page 63

1. Read Exodus 3:1–10.
2. What strikes you most about the story?
3. What questions does it raise in your mind?

188

4. In the Bible, God shows an interest in the political liberation of oppressed people, especially his chosen people. Do you believe God has the same mission today? If so, how should Christians and churches participate in God's mission of political liberation without becoming merely political?

5. What are the main areas of liberation Christians might get involved in?

Chapter 7: A Variety of Religious Oppression

With the coming of Jesus Christ, every law and commandment is turned on its head. They are not ends in themselves but means to an end—a life of freedom and love.

from page 73

1. Read Isaiah 1:12–14; 58:6; Micah 3:9–11; Matthew 23:2–4; Luke 4:18–19; John 8:31–36; Romans 5:12–17; 8:6–8; and Galatians 5:1–6.

2. What strikes you most about these verses?

3. What questions do they raise in your mind?

4. Is the author "proof-texting" here, or is liberation from mere religion a genuine theme running all through Scripture?

5. Where in today's church do you see the greatest temptation to religious oppression?

6. Where in today's church do you see signs of Christ trying to liberate the church from mere religion?

7. What aspect of religion is most oppressive to you personally?

Chapter 8: Jesus the Liberator

[Holy chaos] shatters the order that has become oppressive. It throws out of kilter that which had been tightly controlled.

It forces everyone to make a choice: hold on tighter to a life made in our image, or let go and see the new, liberating thing God is doing.

from page 81

1. Read Mark 3:1–6.
2. What strikes you most about the story?
3. What questions does it raise in your mind?
4. What is most persuasive in the author's interpretation?
5. What is least persuasive?
6. Jesus is shown in this and many other passages as one who deliberately upsets and provokes the established order. Does this aspect of Jesus's ministry excite or disturb you? Why?
7. Jesus is the instigator of holy chaos in this story. As his followers, do we have the duty to do the same? If so, what would that look like? If so, how can we do it without seeming like mere troublemakers?

Chapter 9: Chaos and the Spirit

There is no Christian faith without the institutional church, but the institution is not the Christian faith. The institution is merely the playground in which to enjoy the freedom of God; it is the canvas upon which God paints with broad strokes the miracle of divine love.

from page 85

1. Read Acts 2:1–21.
2. What strikes you most about the story?
3. What questions does it raise in your mind?
4. What is most persuasive in the author's interpretation?
5. What is least persuasive?
6. If the Spirit were to come down mightily on your church today, what sacred assumptions and traditions might be challenged or upset?

Chapter 10: Liberation Starts with Chaos

The work of liberation is God's work first and last. He initiates it. He carries it out. He finishes it. He uses the likes of
Moses, and the likes of us, to do this work. But it is grace
that makes it possible for us to participate in his great work,
and it is God's initiative and power that make it possible for
us to imagine we might even succeed.

from page 95

1. Read Exodus 3 and 4.
2. What strikes you most about the story?
3. What questions does it raise in your mind?
4. What is most persuasive in the author's interpretation?
5. What is least persuasive?
6. Is what ways is Moses's reaction grounded not so much
   in fear as in a desire to stay in control?
7. What are the different liberating works that God might
   be calling you or your church into?
8. How does that call introduce chaos into your life or
   that of your church?

Chapter 11: The Life of Freedom

God's love for us is uncoerced and so freely given that it does
not *demand* a response. But so freely is it given that it creates
freedom in the recipient, so that our response is not one of obligation or duty, nor the returning of a favor, but uncoerced love.

from page 105

1. Read Psalm 51:1; 109:26; Romans 7:15–24; 8:1–11;
   Ephesians 2:4–5.
2. What strikes you most about these verses?
3. What questions do they raise in your mind?
4. Is the author proof-texting here, or does this relationship between love and freedom make sense?

5. If this is true about the relationship of love and freedom, how might this change the way the church does
its ministry?
6. How might it change the way you interact with others?

Chapter 12: From the Horizontal to the Vertical

When you start emphasizing God and what he has done
and will do, well, no telling what will happen. . . . Socially
important and powerful people may start questioning your
relevance, which is another way of saying your sanity. And if
they can't lock you in jail, they may lock you out of their lives.

from page 116

1. In this and subsequent chapters, the author mostly ex-
amines the church in light of themes found in the book
of Acts and the teachings of the New Testament. In
this chapter, what is most persuasive about the author's
interpretation?
2. Where do you see other examples of overemphasis on
the horizontal?
3. What is least persuasive in this chapter?
4. Have you seen examples where there has been an overemphasis on the vertical?
5. Where do you think the balance is in your church?
Should it change?

Chapter 13: From Justice to Grace

I wonder if we're preaching or living the gospel if we don't
scandalize a few listeners, maybe even ourselves, with the
incomprehensible unfairness of it all. When Paul talked about
the gospel, many were shocked and appalled. It sounded as if
God wanted to reward sinners, to give a bonus to scoundrels!

from page 122

1. Do you think the author's comparison between the
AIG bonuses and God's grace to us is a fair one?

2. The author says a major temptation of the church is to be satisfied with reasonable religion. Do you agree? Why or why not?
3. Have you witnessed any examples of the church taming grace?
4. What would grace look like if it was completely unleashed in your church?
5. Would people want that?
6. What would it take for that to happen?

Chapter 14: From Optimism to Resurrection

The resurrection, first and foremost, shows that Jesus is right and we are wrong. He is Lord and we are guilty sinners. To acknowledge this is no small thing, for it means giving up control of one's destiny.

from page 133

1. What are the most prevalent ways we deny death in our culture?
2. Do you agree with the author that even the church can be guilty of denying death? How so?
3. Why isn't the resurrection a more controversial teaching today, something that inspires holy chaos?
4. What needs to most change in the church's teaching and preaching to help people grasp the radical thing that happened in the resurrection?
5. When did the resurrection become a reality for you that profoundly impacted your faith?

Chapter 15: From Marketing to Witness

When the church starts marketing itself or the gospel, something odd is taking place. It subtly turns the free gift of grace into a transaction.

from page 141

1. If we live in a culture saturated with marketing and advertising, what's wrong with the church making use of such techniques to make itself known or the gospel heard?
2. Is it even possible for a church to exist without doing some marketing?
3. What to you are the features of marketing that churches can most readily adapt?
4. What are the features it should avoid?
5. What would be signs that a church is not merely using marketing techniques to make itself known but has actually been co-opted by a marketing mentality?
6. What do you think are the chief differences between marketing the gospel and witnessing to it?

Chapter 16: From Managing to Being Managed

Imagine how freeing it would be to release the death grip we have on our lives and just let the gracious and loving Spirit of Jesus carry us where he would each day.

from page 154

1. Is the megachurch the way the church has adapted to a particular culture, or is it mostly a perversion of what the church is about?
2. What to you are the biggest benefits of the megachurch?
3. What are its biggest drawbacks?
4. What to you are the worst ways churches large and small try to manage ministry instead of being managed by the Holy Spirit?
5. Does being managed by the Spirit mean we abandon church programs and planning?
6. What might it look like for a church to be more managed by the Spirit?

Chapter 17: From Shame to Obedience

Whenever we wrestle with the Spirit like this, we wrestle with that original sin: the desire to order our lives, the yearning to control the shape of our existence.

from page 162

1. Have you had an experience like the author's, where you felt the nudging of the Holy Spirit? Did you balk or follow through? What happened?
2. How do you discern the difference between the leading of the Spirit and your own fanciful thoughts?
3. Some Christians say they never have a sense of the Spirit's leading. Is this something that needs to happen to every Christian? Are there other ways to be "led by the Spirit" that are less intuitive?
4. What do you think are the biggest dangers of trying to be sensitive to the Spirit in these very personal ways?
5. What is the biggest temptation in your church—to get carried away with personal encounters with the Spirit, or to ignore that dimension of faith all together?

Chapter 18: From Power to Promise

The paradox is that we really have to abandon all desire for change—that is, all desire to control and order a new life for ourselves or for our society—before any significant change can occur.

from page 170

1. Do North American Christians have too high an expectation of how God can change them or their churches? Or too low an expectation?
2. What types of things can God change in a person in this life?

3. What is the difference between the change that the gospel says it will work in us and the changes that most self-help groups offer?
4. What types of changes must we wait to experience in the next life?
5. If you were to put transformation on a scale of 1 (no change) to 100 (complete change), how much transformation can we expect in this life?
6. What are the biggest problems with overestimating how much change we can experience in this life?
7. What are the biggest problems with underestimating it?

Chapter 19: From Utopia to Church

We want to start pulling at the weeds, or at least spray some Roundup. I suspect Jesus knew that if we started controlling weeds, we'd end up killing ourselves.

from page 179

1. What aspects of the church's life do you find most troubling or embarrassing?
2. If Christ knew this would be how the church would turn out, why do you suppose he founded it in the first place?
3. Do you agree with the author that we should love others without imposing our expectations on them? Are there any expectations we can impose that would be intrinsically loving?
4. What areas in your church's life need the most improving?
5. In which of those can you realistically hope for significant change?
6. Which do you need to accept in grace and forgiveness?

196

Epilogue

Our maturity in Christ comes not from playing it safe.

from page 184

1. Thinking about the whole book, what to you was most convincing and/or helpful?
2. What questions does it leave you with?
3. What are you going to do differently as a result of reading and discussing this book?

NOTES

Introduction

1. Walter Brueggemann, *Genesis*, Interpretation series (Atlanta: John Knox Press, 1980), 16.

2. This brief essay can be found in many anthologies, including *Provocations: Spiritual Writing of Kierkegaard*, ed. Charles Moore (Maryknoll, NY: Orbis, 2003), and online at http://www.philosophicalfragments.com/?page_id=13.

3. The commentaries I've found most helpful are Beverly Roberts Gaventa, *Acts*, Abingdon New Testament Commentary series (Nashville: Abingdon, 2003); William Willimon, *Acts*, Interpretation series (Louisville: Westminster John Knox Press, 2010); and Ben Witherington III, *The Acts of the Apostles: A Socio-Rhetorical Commentary* (Grand Rapids: Eerdmans, 1998).

Chapter 1 The Religious Captivity of the Church

1. This originally appeared in *Esquire* magazine and now can be found in the anthology *Esquire—The Meaning of Life: Wit, Wisdom, and Wonder from 65 Extraordinary People*, ed. Brendan Vaughan (New York: Hearst Communications, 2004), 91.

2. Bruce Sheiman, *An Atheist Defends Religion: Why Humanity Is Better Off with Religion than Without It* (New York: Alpha Books, 2009).

3. Robert D. Putnam and David E. Campbell, *American Grace: How Religion Divides and Unites Us* (New York: Simon and Schuster, 2010).

4. Michael Gerson, "A Faith for The Nones: The Right Kind of Religion Would Bring the Young Back," *Washington Post*, May 8, 2009, http://www.washingtonpost.com/wp-dyn/content/article/2009/05/07/AR2009050703056_pf.html.

5. For a fine analysis of how the suburbs shape us in all sorts of ways, see David Goetz, *Death by Suburb: How to Keep the Suburbs from Killing Your Soul* (New York: HarperOne, 2007).

6. Annie Dillard, "An Expedition to the Pole," in *Teaching a Stone to Talk*, rev. ed. (New York: Harper Perennial, 1988), 52–53.

7. Dorothy L. Sayers, "The Greatest Drama Ever Staged," in *Christian Letters to a Post-Christian World: A Selection of Essays* (Grand Rapids: Eerdmans, 1969), 15.

Chapter 2 The Eucatastrophe

1. The assumption of the Genesis narrative is the existence of a world as we know it—fully formed, resplendent with life in all its forms. The account is not a primitive attempt to describe evolution, nor a naïve, literal description of how everything came to be. First and foremost it is a theological narrative—a story to tell us about God and his ways. And the fully formed world from which the narrator writes is the context of the narrative. My interpretive move is to take this one step further and use the present shape of our lived existence as a repeated point of contrast, to highlight one particular theological theme I find in this chapter, and actually in all of Scripture.

Chapter 3 Another Eucatastrophe

1. See Genesis 2:16–17. As in the last chapter, this chapter will be grounded in Genesis 2 and 3 but without repeatedly noting all specific references.

The careful reader will note my indebtedness to the early church father Irenaeus, especially chapters 20, 23, 38 of Book III, and chapters 37 and 38 of Book IV of his *Against Heresies*. See http://www.ccel.org/ccel/schaff/anf01.toc.html for the table of contents, and click on chapter titles to read specific chapters.

The main idea I take from Irenaeus is that "the fall" was neither an unexpected nor an unmitigated disaster. It was a combination of human weakness and pride, but hardly something that shocked or surprised God. In fact, it appears to be something God allowed in order to bring the crown of his creation to ultimate maturity and freedom in Christ: "God thus determining all things beforehand for the bringing of man to perfection, for his edification, and for the revelation of his dispensations, that goodness may both be made apparent, and righteousness perfected, and that the church may be fashioned after the image of his Son, and that man may finally be brought to maturity at some future time, becoming ripe through such privileges to see and comprehend God" (Book IV, chapter 37).

2. Aristotle, *Politics*, Book 1, Chapter V, available online at http://en.wikisource.org/wiki/Politics_%28Aristotle%29/Book_1.

3. Of course, the reference is to the Beatitudes, Matthew 5:1–11, and to the suffering and death of Jesus himself. One of the deep mysteries of life is that God turns weakness into strength and death into life.

Chapter 6 Early Signs of Liberation

1. George Orwell, *Nineteen Eighty-Four* (New York: Plume Books, 1983), 277.

Chapter 7 A Variety of Religious Oppression

1. See Matthew 6, where Jesus instructs his followers on how to perform these practices, but never argues for them. He merely assumes that his followers will be engaged with them.

2. See especially Isaiah 44:9–17, one of the funniest passages in the Bible.

Chapter 8 Jesus the Liberator

1. See the Sermon on the Mount (Matt. 5–7) and passages like Mark 10:17–31.

Chapter 10 Liberation Starts with Chaos

1. Martin Luther King, Jr., "Letter from a Birmingham Jail," April 16, 1963. This letter can be found in many places, among others the website of the African American Studies Department at the University of Pennsylvania, http://www. africa.upenn.edu/Articles_Gen/Letter_Birmingham.html.

2. This phrase Bonhoeffer attributes to Gottfried Arnold. The entire quote is from *Life Together* (San Francisco: HarperSanFrancisco, 1978), 99.

3. "John Brown's Speech to the Court at His Trial," November 2, 1859, as found online at the National Center for Public Policy, http://www.nationalcenter. org/JohnBrown%27sSpeech.html.

Chapter 12 From the Horizontal to the Vertical

1. Flannery O'Connor, *Wise Blood* (New York: Farrar, Straus and Giroux, 2007), 157.

2. Wade Clark Roof, *Spiritual Marketplace: Baby Boomers and the Remaking of American Religion* (Princeton, NJ: Princeton University Press, 1999), 129.

3. Ibid.

4. Christian Smith with Melinda Lundquist Denton, *Soul Searching: The Religious and Spiritual Lives of American Teenagers* (New York: Oxford University Press, 2005).

5. Ibid., 162–63.

6. Ibid., 162.

7. Alexis de Tocqueville, *Democracy in America*, trans. Henry Reeve (Stilwell, KS: Digireads.com, 2007), 23, emphasis added.

8. "A Call to Spiritual Formation," June 2009, San Antonio, Texas, http:// acalltospiritualformation.info/default.aspx.

9. Soong Chan Rah, *The Next Evangelicalism: Freeing the Church from Western Cultural Captivity* (Downers Grove, IL: InterVarsity Press, 2009), 160.

10. Following Jesus website, http://followingjesus.org/.

11. Brian D. McLaren, homepage, "Dr. David Dunbar Gets It Right," December 19, 2008, http://www.brianmclaren.net/archives/blog/dr-david-dunbar-gets-it-right.html.

12. Roof, *Spiritual Marketplace*, 129.

13. Martin Luther, "The Freedom of the Christian," in *Three Treatises* (Philadelphia: Fortress Press, 1970), 279.

Chapter 13 From Justice to Grace

1. David Stout, "A.I.G. Chief Asks Bonus Recipients to Give Back Half," *New York Times*, March 18, 2009, http://www.nytimes.com/2009/03/19/business/19web-aig.html?_r=1&8au&emc=au.

Chapter 14 From Optimism to Resurrection

1. Ernst Becker, *The Denial of Death* (New York: Free Press, 1997), xvii.
2. Søren Kierkegaard, *Either/Or*, trans. Howard Hong and Edna Hong (Princeton, NJ: Princeton University Press, 1987), 20.
3. Rob Stein, "Daily Red Meat Raises Chances of Dying Early: Study Is First Large Analysis of Link with Overall Health," *Washington Post*, March 24, 2009, http://www.washingtonpost.com/wp-dyn/content/article/2009/03/23/AR2009032301626.html.
4. Karen Kaplan, "Aligning a Medical Treatment Plan with God's Plan: Faith Drives Some Patients to Fight, and Suffer More at the End," *Los Angeles Times*, March 18, 2009, http://articles.latimes.com/2009/mar/18/science/sci-faith18.
5. Dietrich Bonhoeffer, *The Cost of Discipleship*, trans. R. H. Fuller and Irmgard Booth (New York: Simon & Schuster, 1995), 89.

Chapter 15 From Marketing to Witness

1. Rob Moll, "Saved by an Atheist," *Christianity Today*, August 25, 2010, http://www.christianitytoday.com/ct/2010/august/28.40.html.

Chapter 16 From Managing to Being Managed

1. I recognize the exegetical problem with the phrase "the city of Samaria" (that is, the major city in Samaria at the time was called Sebaste—see Beverly Gaventa, *Acts*, in Abingdon New Testament Commentary series [Nashville: Abingdon Press, 2003], 136). But I will go with the preponderance of manuscripts, which read this way. Luke could be referring to the city by its former name or trying to emphasize the Samaritan-ness of the locale.
2. I like the way Beverly Gaventa put it: "The force of the command lies in its very absurdity, since God commands what is unexpected, even what is ridiculous." Gaventa, *Acts*, 141.
3. From an email received on August 10, 2009, for the Worship Facilities Conference & Expo scheduled to take place October 27–30, 2009, in Charlotte, North Carolina.
4. All the quotes below are from Scott Thumma's paper titled *Exploring the Megachurch Phenomena: Their Characteristics and Cultural Context* (Hartford, CT: Hartford Institute for Religion Research, 1996), which can be found on the Hartford Institute for Religion Research website at http://hirr.hartsem.edu/bookshelf/thumma_article2.html.

Chapter 17 From Shame to Obedience

1. David Bebbington, *Evangelicalism in Modern Britain: A History from the 1730s to the 1980s* (Oxford: Routledge, 1989).

Chapter 18 From Power to Promise

1. There is some question as to how these Samaritan believers could be baptized and not have received the Holy Spirit—as if Luke is saying, contrary to Peter's affirmation in Acts 2:38, that faith and baptism do not confer the Holy Spirit. Naturally, opinions vary as to what Luke is saying here, but perhaps Luke is merely talking about an extraordinary reception of the Spirit (the "falling" of the Spirit), one that is manifested in unusual signs and wonders. This is not a gift given to all believers, nor is it required of all believers. But when it is given, it is a sign of the power and grace of God for all who experience and witness it.

2. Michael Horton, *Christless Christianity: The Alternative Gospel of the American Church* (Grand Rapids: Baker, 2008), 94.

3. Ibid.

4. Karl Barth, *The Epistle to the Romans*, trans. Edwyn C. Hoskins, 6th ed. (New York: Oxford University Press, 1968), 163.

5. As quoted in Gene Edward Veith, *A Place to Stand: The Word of God in the Life of Martin Luther* (Nashville: Cumberland House, 2005), 163.

6. As quoted in Alister McGrath, *Iustitia Dei: A History of the Christian Doctrine of Justification*, 3rd ed. (Cambridge: Cambridge University Press, 2006), 228.

Chapter 19 From Utopia to Church

1. John Winthrop, "A Model of Christian Charity," speech given on the *Arbella* in 1630, as found on the Religious Freedom Page website at http://religiousfreedom.lib.virginia.edu/sacred/charity.html.

2. "The Result of the 1679 General Synod," taken from Williston Walker, *The Creeds and Platforms of Congregationalism* (Boston, 1893), 423–31, available online at http://www.swarthmore.edu/SocSci/bdorsey1/41docs/34-jer.html.

3. David Kinnaman and Gabe Lyons, *unChristian: What a New Generation Really Thinks about Christianity . . . and Why It Matters* (Grand Rapids: Baker, 2007).

4. Julia Duin, *Quitting Church: Why the Faithful Are Fleeing and What to Do About It* (Grand Rapids: Baker, 2008).

5. Larry Crabb, *Real Church: Does It Exist? Can I Find It?* (Nashville: Thomas Nelson, 2009).

6. Ibid., 154.

Mark Galli is senior managing editor of *Christianity Today* and author of the biweekly column Soulwork. A former Presbyterian minister, he is the author, coauthor, or editor of several books, including *Jesus Mean and Wild*, *Beyond Smells and Bells*, and *Francis of Assisi and His World*. He lives in Glen Ellyn, Illinois.

God loves you and has a difficult plan for your life.

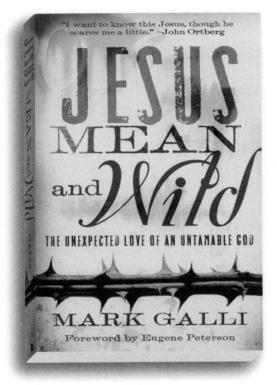

"I want to know this Jesus, though he scares me a little." –John Ortberg

JESUS MEAN and Wild

THE UNEXPECTED LOVE OF AN UNTAMABLE GOD

MARK GALLI

Foreword by Eugene Peterson

Encountering the attributes of God makes a difference in how we relate to him.

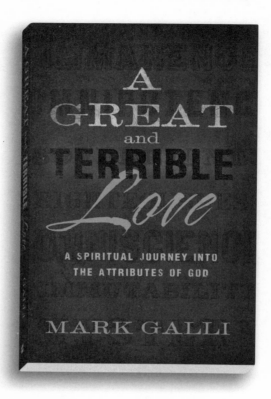

Too often, we make God too small, too manageable. But careful examination of God's attributes reveals a God full of mystery, eternity, righteousness, and mercy. In *A Great and Terrible Love*, Mark Galli thoughtfully delivers unexpected glimpses into fifteen classic attributes of God, exposing cheap substitutes and delivering a fresh vision of God.

"The book you hold now is a part of the longest and most important conversation held by the human race: What is God like?"—from the foreword by John Ortberg

BakerBooks

Relevant. Intelligent. Engaging.

Available in bookstores, online at www.bakerbooks.com, or by calling (800) 877-2665.
Like us on ￼ Follow us on ￼ ReadBakerBooks Baker Book Blog: relligent.wordpress.com